Dream Big!

What's the Best That Can Happen?

A Spiritual Guide to Unlimited Possibilities

Barbara Sanfilippo

Make It Happen Press
Escondido, California

Although the author and publisher have made every effort to ensure the accuracy and completeness of information contained in this book, we assume no responsibility for errors, inaccuracies, omissions, or any inconsistency herein. Any slights of people, places, or organizations are unintentional.

First printing 1999
Second printing 2001

ISBN 0-9669215-4-2

LCCN 99-93039

ATTENTION CORPORATIONS, UNIVERSITIES, COLLEGES, CHARITIES, AND PROFESSIONAL ORGANIZATIONS: Quantity discounts are available on bulk purchases of this book for premiums, gifts, or educational purposes. We welcome fund raising and sponsorship opportunities with charities. Special books or book excerpts can also be created to fit specific needs. For information, please contact Make It Happen Press, 2421 Oak Canyon Place, Escondido, CA 92025, (760) 738-9100.

APPLAUSE FOR *DREAM BIG!*

Dream Big! shows you how to take your foot off the brakes and accelerate your goals and make them into realities. This is a self-help manual that is turbo-charged with power tools for success. It can and will change your life!

Willie Jolley, Author
It Only Takes a Minute to Change Your Life

Barbara Sanfilippo shows conclusively that God helps those who help themselves. And then she shows how to do that.

Alan Weiss, Ph.D., Author *Million Dollar Consulting*

Barbara's "Dream Big!" message is powerful, practical and proven. I enjoyed it just as much as having her speak in person to my managers and staff. A must read for anyone who wants to take charge of their life. Barbara is a practitioner of her own "Big Dreams!" and lives her life accordingly, which makes her book refreshingly credible and honest.

Mike Maslak, President North Island Federal Credit Union

Barbara Sanfilippo is a rare speaker who shares practical ideas for living a full, purposeful life. *Dream Big!* is her gift you don't want to miss.

John Fridlington, CAE, Vice President
California Association of REALTORS®

If you apply Barbara's techniques described in this book, you will live every day with more purpose and joy.

Marcia Wieder, Author *Doing Less and Having More*

Dream Big! offers an exciting action plan of how to take your desires and turn them into reality What a fantastic road map for living.

Tom Antion, Author *Wake 'em Up Business Presentations*

I got amazing results with her Dream Big board--try it and watch out! Can't wait to get copies of Barbara's book for my friends.

Marilyn Schott, National Speaker, Trainer

This book is dedicated with
deepest love and affection
to my sweetie and husband,
Bob Romano.
His love, support, strength and "anything
is possible" attitude have inspired me to
always expect the best.

■ ■ ■

Experience Barbara Live!

You can have Barbara present her powerful Dream Big message or another appropriate topic at your company meeting, sales conference or association convention. Alternatively, get your own group together for a private workshop with Barbara. Consider splitting expenses with several other businesses or organizations. As she travels throughout the United States and Canada she will be in your area soon.

For information on our speaking, training, consulting or management retreat services call us at: 1-877-I Succeed or email us at Barb@Romanosanfilippo.com or contact your favorite speaker's bureau. Please check out Barbara's Web page at www. RomanoSanfilippo.com.

ACKNOWLEDGEMENTS

Seeing this book in print is a dream come true for me—a BIG DREAM. It is the culmination of years of hard work and persistence filled with both discouraging and rewarding moments. Fortunately, many people encouraged me to make this book happen and they deserve a special thank you.

My biggest thank you is to you, Lord, for always being there for me and guiding me daily on this project. You spoke and I listened to your wise counsel. When Bob and I came very close to losing our home in the devastating Oakland fire I made you a promise. I said if you spared our house I would use my speaking and writing talents to draw people to you and remind them of your awesome power and love. When I returned after the evacuation and saw our house untouched in the midst of hundreds of charred houses, I knew you took me up on my offer. DREAM BIG! is the fulfillment of my promise to you.

I'd like to thank my optimistic mom who always says, "Go for it" and my deceased dad for always telling me I'm smart and can do anything. My sister, Patricia, has been an angel and guiding light shining constantly for me.

I'm honored to be a member of the National Speakers Association. Without the support of my peers, this book would never have been born. NSA has taught me everything I know about publishing and speaking. To all my friends at NSA, thank you so much for generously sharing your time, knowledge and experiences.

To all my friends and associates who patiently listened and saw me through the ups and downs of this project. Your encouragement helped me stay sane and not give up. A special thank you to Cynthia Schneider, Kyle Roat, Marsha Ruben, Dace Swenson, Nina Katz, Mary Marcdante and Padi Selwyn.

Many individuals have generously given their time and experiences by contributing their personal stories in this book. Thank you Katie Quinn, Padi Selwyn, Mary Marcdante, Tim Schwartz, Mike Maslak, Marianna Nunes, Elaine Speece, Marilyn Schott, Dayle Dunn, Carl Mehler and Jim Cathcart. The movie "Rudy" inspired me greatly and I'm honored to have Rudy Ruettiger do the foreword for this book. To all those who took the time to review my book and write an endorsement— thank you.

My incredibly efficient, dedicated and patient staff, Janet Berry and Judy Norris, deserve special recognition. Thank you for tirelessly typing, editing, proofing and coordinating all the details of this project with a smile.

I'm grateful for my speaking, training and consulting clients who've given me the opportunity to learn, grow and share my thoughts. Seeing the positive results with your audience, staff performance or overall corporate culture has been rewarding. Thanks to all of my audience attendees for enthusiastically embracing my message and taking the time to write or phone with your words of praise.

Thank you Carol Susan Roth for helping me shape and clarify my six step "make it happen" process. Hats off to Marilyn Ross and the great staff at About Books, Inc. for literally coordinating every detail of this book including: cover design, layout, editing, promotional copy, printing, moral support and much more.

And a final thank you to you, my reader, for buying this book and allowing me to partner with you to make your dreams happen.

FOREWORD

by RUDY REUTTIGER
(The inspiration behind the TriStar
blockbuster hit movie RUDY)

Congratulations—you're in for a big treat. *DREAM BIG! What's the Best That Can Happen?* is a gold mine filled with practical ideas and a game plan you can follow to achieve your dreams. You'll have fun reading the inspiring stories and doing the creative exercises.

What I really like about this book is how Barbara encourages us to tap into our spiritual side to create action and get results. It's the kind of book you'll refer to again and again for guidance and inspiration. Barbara discusses her "act as if" principle where she tells us to make believe our dream is coming true and prepare for it. My dream of going to Notre Dame and playing on the football team happened because of visualization, preparation and persistence. First I saw myself there, then I took action steps to prepare for it—steps that would get me closer to my dream...and through persistence, I never quit! I used the same success principles to get the movie RUDY made in Hollywood and to become a motivational speaker around the world today.

Barbara writes like she speaks. Her words are filled with contagious energy, enthusiasm, and encouragement. Corporations and audiences around the world enjoy her powerful and entertaining message. Sales teams, CEOs and individuals use her techniques to create proven results in both their personal and professional life. When you read *DREAM BIG! What's the Best That Can Happen?* you have Barbara as your very own personal dream consultant.

Go for it!

Rudy Ruettiger

TABLE OF CONTENTS

INTRODUCTION

I love watching the expression on people's faces when they ask what I do. I typically answer, "I'm a professional speaker and a dream coach. I help people Dream Big." This gets their attention. "You mean you can actually teach someone to dream? How?" they ask with a mixture of doubt and excitement. So I give it a shot and try to offer some words of wisdom. This book is really the "how"—all tied up and neat in one little package.

Imagine feeling like every day is your birthday or Christmas. Beautifully wrapped gifts are waiting to be opened. A wonderful surprise is waiting for you in each box, and each package represents a different aspect of your life. One may be your work, another love, or perhaps your spiritual life. It's such an exciting feeling. That's how I view my life. It wasn't always that way, however, since I had a rather difficult childhood and challenges to overcome. We all face challenges and obstacles. Despite these challenges I somehow found the courage to pursue my dreams. You'll read about some of the fears, disappointments, wonderful surprises, and good fortune, I and many others experienced along the way.

Every one of us has hopes and dreams. You do. I do. For years I've been sharing my Dream Big message with audiences around the world. Many of my friends have told me, "Barbara, you have a talent for creating everything that you want. You imagine a dream and then it just happens." I get numerous letters from people in my audiences who write, "I tried your suggestions and you won't believe what happened." With excitement they write about their wonderful new relationship, dream job, or new house.

I guess some people think I'm lucky or have a magic wand. The truth is I don't believe in luck or magic. But I do believe in persistence, hard work, and imagination, so I decided to go back and reflect on all my successes and dreams. What did I do to attract my wonderful husband? To become a professional speaker and author? How did we create our beautiful dream home? How did we find the courage to work through all the disappointments and fears? And you know what? I discovered that over and over again I was using a simple, six-step process. Six simple steps plus a touch of faith and spirituality for good measure.

This book is for you if:

- You are frustrated with your job or career but can't seem to take the next step.
- You would like to create a satisfying long-term relationship or improve the one you currently have.
- You have ever said to yourself, "There must be more to life."
- You feel like you're making a living and not living your life.
- You want to attract prosperity and happiness in your life.

■ You want to embrace your spiritual side and deepen your faith.

■ You want to begin celebrating and appreciating all the blessings you currently have.

■ You want to overcome obstacles and fears that hold you back from achieving your full potential.

■ You want to find time to enjoy yourself and play more.

■ You want to learn how to Dream Big and make it happen!

I want to share my six-step, *make it happen* process with you. You deserve to live a life filled with love, joy, success, and prosperity. It's no accident you are reading this book. Right now your dreams are waiting to happen. Yes, you heard me correctly. I repeat, they're *waiting to happen.* All you need to do is be open-minded and willing to do the necessary work and preparation. Please allow me to be your personal dream coach and show you how easy it is to Dream Big.

Dream Big is a proven action plan to create powerful results in your life. Although this book is intentionally small and simple to read, you can expect BIG results. It is designed as a six-week program. When you get to the six-step *make it happen* process, I encourage you to review and practice one step each week. At the end of six weeks you'll understand exactly how to Dream Big. Please understand it may take one week, one year, or ten years to manifest your dream; rest assured, however, it is in process. All you have to do is keep *acting as if* (described in Step 6) and use the bonus tips for the spiritually inclined at the end of each section.

This book does not focus on achieving material success, although I'll show you how, if you like. Who wouldn't want to take a nice vacation now and then, live in a lovely home, and be able to afford the nicer things in life? That's a given. It's really a question of how happy you feel within: the quality of your relationships with your family and friends; the leisure time you have to truly enjoy yourself and experience the beauty all around you in nature and people; and most important, that you are filling your divine purpose—the essence of why you are here. Making sure you are contributing by helping others and living a life of gratitude.

This book is much more than a personal improvement plan. It is also a spiritual guide to ease your journey. Therefore, I do use the word God, or the Lord, occasionally. If this is uncomfortable for you, please feel free to use your own word to acknowledge your spiritual source. If you do not believe in a higher power, skip the optional Tips for the Spiritually Inclined at the end of each step. You will still get some results. However, those of you who practice the six steps and also embrace the spiritual tips, buckle your seat belt and hold on tight. In fact, I've added a special section at the end, Message for the Spiritually Inclined.

The exercises are critical to getting the maximum results. They are designed to help you take in the words and *feel* them—to bring them alive. It's been proven that people who can imagine with real *emotion* are much more likely to achieve their dreams. In addition, the exercises will help you identify any obstacles that may be getting in your way.

If you choose to simply read the book and skip the exercises, you can expect minimal results. You may prefer to read the entire book quickly in a day or two and then go back and do the exercises over six weeks. Or you can complete the exercises before going on to the next step. Either method is fine as long as you do the work.

Many people have found it helpful to create a Dream Big support group with a small gathering of friends. For years I met monthly with a group of my friends. The purpose of our group was to help one another achieve our dreams. At each meeting we took turns discussing a principle from a favorite book and how we could use the ideas. Then each one of us stated a dream or a fear and asked for encouragement. We ended each session by imagining we each had our dream. It was a tremendous success.

By meeting periodically with your own Dream Big group, you're likely to stay focused and avoid discouragement. Although practicing the six steps is fairly simple, the timing of your results depends on your unique situation and readiness. It's quite exciting as over time you get to celebrate a group member's success. I strongly recommend you create a Dream Big support group. If you're not the group type, at least find one Dream Big partner. For more information see the Invitation to Join the Big Dream Club in the back of the book. Sales professionals may also consider joining the Big Dream Sales Club.

To get the most out of this book, you'll need to buy a spiral bound notebook, and use it throughout the book, as directed. Your Dream Big workbook will become a valuable tool and your personal "bible" to guide you to your destination. Carry it with you and read it often.

By reading *Dream Big!* discover how to:

■ Live a life of joy and abundance.

■ Work through fears and accelerate forward.

■ Get guidance and inspiration daily.

■ Keep your dream alive and avoid discouragement.

■ Determine what's really important.

■ Enjoy life more and with less effort.

■ Use the easy, six-step *make it happen* process to create powerful results.

■ Live with gratitude and in the spirit of service.

■ Develop your spirituality to experience the happiness you deserve.

Are you ready to have your heart's desires? Do you have the courage, persistence, and commitment to ask, "What's the best that can happen?" Dream Big is a guide to live life fully with a six-step process that will change your life forever. It is my gift to you—enjoy!

PART I

What's The Best That Can Happen?

7

Expect the Best—
You Deserve It!

Don't be afraid that your life will end;
be afraid that it will never begin.
—Grace Hansen

Back when I was single, I went on a date with a guy named Rob. The conversation at dinner was lively and stimulating until I began talking about houses. At the time, I rented a small but charming studio in the Marina District of San Francisco and shared with Rob my dream of one day owning a nice home in the Bay Area. He quickly responded, "Are you kidding? With the price of homes in California, I'll never own a home." He then went on to point out all the reasons why it was useless to even think of having a home since he would never have one. That was my last date with Rob.

Even though I had absolutely no money at the time to buy a house, I expected to own one in the future. Rob, on the other hand, admitted he wanted a house but would never have one. It suddenly hit me. Some people expect the best, some expect the worst, and sadly, some don't expect anything at all. What about you? What do you expect?

I want to introduce you to a proven six-step process I've developed that will help you expect the best and get it too. Just as soil and plants must be fertilized and prepped to grow healthy, your mind needs to be prepared for great things. Let's begin by examining your current attitudes and beliefs.

Do You Believe It's Possible?

It's important to open up your mind to believe it's possible to have your dreams. No matter what your age or current circumstances, it's still possible. I assume you want to live a joyful and fulfilling life. However, this may require some preparation. If you've experienced some disappointments, frustrations, and pain in the past, I understand why you may be afraid to get your hopes up.

Let me state right now a basic truth I'm sure you've heard before. If you can't *imagine* something or believe it's even *possible*, there's little chance you'll have it. Please note, I said *imagine it*. I didn't say you *have it* yet. In other words, do you allow yourself the luxury and pleasure of filling your mind with incredible pictures of your future?

If you've ever had a pleasant daydream or seen yourself in a scene you created, you have what it takes to Dream Big. The key question is, do you *believe* and *expect* to get it? Or do you dismiss it as idle thoughts? Many people daydream and imagine wonderful things only to say, "Who am I kidding? I'll never have X." Therefore, the only difference between those who live a life of joy and those who live a life of struggle are the three words *belief, faith* and *action*. They *believe* in their dreams, have *faith* it will happen, and take *action*.

For instance, my friend Katie always expects the best. She had a wonderful job as an administrative assistant at a research company in the San Francisco area but decided to live and work in the wine country in the Sonoma/Napa Valley area. This required picking up, moving to a new area, and starting her life over. Although there were many obstacles to overcome, Katie focused on the best. Listen to her story:

> I had saved some money in anticipation of moving, storage, and so forth. I took five months off and did some traveling, then decided it was time to look for my dream job. I wanted to be an assistant to a winery executive. I enjoy wine and the idea of working at a winery was just ideal to me. I was very clear in my head about that and made that clear to the four employment agencies I signed up with—all telling me that I would never make the salary I was making in Silicon Valley; all telling me I would probably have to start at the bottom somewhere to get my foot in the door and work my way up. I'm over forty and I didn't feel I needed to work my way up!
>
> I did a couple of temp jobs and had a couple of interviews. At this point I was low on cash and was offered positions at two companies. One was a winery; one was in an educational facility. I was tempted to take one of them just to get the cash flow moving again. The winery position wanted to pay me a salary I was making twenty years ago! The educational facility position turned out to be run by a group of individuals who were very disorganized. I turned them both down, because I knew the salary range I was worth and I knew the type of people I wanted to work with and decided not to compromise on that, even if it meant holding out longer on obtaining my dream job...meanwhile, the cash pot was getting smaller and smaller.
>
> Three days after deciding not to take the positions, I got a phone call from one of the agencies asking if I was available to temp for a winery executive. I, OF COURSE, said yes. The agency told me the winery would be filling the position per-

manently. As the goose bumps rose on my arms, I was very excited about this prospect. After a couple of days in this winery, I knew I wanted the position. Everything about the job was perfect for me. Within four weeks, I was offered the position—making more money than I was making in Silicon Valley.

I was willing to hold out until I got what I wanted, expected, and deserved. I would not settle for anything less. I am so happy and I sometimes think what my frame of mind would be if I took those other jobs!! YUCK. You get what you settle for. Try settling for the best—it's much more rewarding, empowering, and fun. If you settle for less, that is exactly what you will get.

The only difference between those who live a life of joy and those who live a life of struggle are three words: belief, faith, *and* action.

Don't Settle for the Status Quo

Many of us are reluctant to use our imagination and are afraid to Dream Big. After all, we don't want to be disappointed. Content with the status quo, we may settle for a life of mediocrity. Perhaps there's an underlying feeling we don't deserve happiness. Or maybe we bought into the myth that life is supposed to be tough, and we should grin and bear it. This is *limited* thinking. I want to get you in the habit of *unlimited* thinking.

It's time to lay the groundwork to help you open up to possibilities and imagine the best. It's important to build a foundation before you learn the six-step process. Now it's time to get to work and warm up with some exercises. Remember, the exercises are going to accelerate your results so take the time to invest in yourself.

Summary of Key Points

■ Examine your current attitude. Do you expect the best, the worst or nothing at all?

■ Believe it's possible to have your dreams, and have faith it will happen.

■ Use your imagination and Dream Big.

■ Ask for guidance daily.

Exercise: Life Satisfaction Index

Before you can move forward, let's assess where you are now. The following Life Satisfaction Index (LSI) is included to help you identify what's important. To prepare for the dream process, rate how satisfied you are with the following areas of your life on a scale of 1 to 5 with 5 being very satisfied and 1 being the "pits." (Circle your selection.)

Life Satisfaction Index					
1. Work/Career	1	2	3	4	5
2. Personal Relationships/Love	1	2	3	4	5
3. Parent/Family Life	1	2	3	4	5
4. Relaxation/Social Time	1	2	3	4	5
5. Spiritual	1	2	3	4	5
6. Physical Fitness/Health	1	2	3	4	5
7. Financial	1	2	3	4	5
8. Personal Growth/Education	1	2	3	4	5
9. Service to Others	1	2	3	4	5

Exercise: Areas for Opportunity

Let's get to work in your personal Dream Big workbook. At the top of a blank page, write the date and Areas for Improvement and Growth in My Life. Now look at your Life Satisfaction Index and note the most important areas you wish to improve. These may not necessarily be items with the lowest score.

Feel free to list as many as you choose, but it helps to prioritize and focus on one or two for now. Next to each one, also jot down what you "expect" to happen and an action step. For example:

Area of Improvement	Action
I'd like to improve my relationship with my husband. I expect the best as we grow closer and more loving by communicating our feelings and spending more quality time together.	Suggest a marriage retreat
I'd like to improve my financial affairs so I can retire early and in comfort.	Make larger payments on my credit cards and use them less. See a financial planner to create a budget and review my current mutual funds.

Exercise: Ask for Guidance

To begin tapping into your power supply, ask for guidance. In your workbook, write a one- or two-sentence prayer or affirmation to improve your lowest score. For example:

■ "Dear Lord or _____, Thank you for your guidance in helping me get my financial affairs in order and for all the abundance in my life."

■ "I am now enjoying my leisure time and balanced lifestyle with family and friends."

■ Write your own prayer or affirmation now for each of your lowest scores.

Review these periodically and say them with meaning and expectation. I know this may be difficult; however, in Step 1 you'll have an opportunity to identify any obstacles preventing you from believing your dreams.

Message for the Spiritually Inclined

To prepare for all the good coming your way, repeat the following affirmation frequently or as needed. Please fill in the name of your spiritual source. I prefer to use God or the Lord, but you should use whatever feels best for you. Of course, I encourage you to always create your own affirmation or prayer.

I expect the best and say "yes" to all the blessings coming to me.

■ ■ ■

I am enthusiastic about life! Something is rising within me and shining out from me. It is my enthusiasm for life! I am alive with the life of God, and I am excited about all the possibilities that are before me! Never before and never again will I have the same opportunities that today will bring, so I look forward to each moment of the day as a new adventure—a new adventure in loving, a new adventure in unfolding to my unlimited potential.

—Excerpted from the *Daily Word*

■ ■ ■

I do not doubt that God or _____ created me to be happy, so how could I ever doubt that I have all I need to live my life to the fullest? I do not doubt God! So as the day begins, I give thanks for the blessings I already have and get ready for the new blessings in store for me!

■ ■ ■

I have the opportunity for many gifts today. I hope I see them.

—Anne Wilson Schaef

PART II

Discover The Six-Step *Make It Happen* Process

Step 1: Welcome Wake-Up Calls–

Pay Attention to the Guiding Signs

> *Problems are messages.*
> —Shakti Gawain

Judy is a marketing representative I met many years ago in my previous life as a sales rep. Despite the fact that she made a comfortable living, she was always creating financial crises in her life. Just when she got things under control with a debt management plan or a higher paying job another crisis popped up. Once she loaned money to a new boyfriend who quietly disappeared. Then she invested in a friend's business she knew nothing about. After many years on this roller coaster she finally got it. Judy was addicted to "living on the edge" and ignoring her wake-up calls. Once she accepted responsibility that her experiences were not bad luck but self-created, she began to make dramatic improvements.

I have good news. Once you decide to Dream Big you will get all kinds of cues and signals to let you know when you are *on course* or *off course*. I call these *wake-up calls*.

Step 1 of the *make it happen* process is to welcome and identify those wake-up calls. This first week we'll take a look at why we sometimes ignore obvious signs guiding us on the journey of life. Content to drive along at the same old speed, we may have a passive attitude and resist change. "This is my life—I guess I'll make the best of it." "Life is tough—there's nothing I can do."

In addition, we may not know what we want out of life. In essence we are blocked and have no dreams, hopes or burning desires, which are essential to creating our future reality. Or we may have dreams, but we keep creating obstacles and sabotaging our own efforts.

Wake-Up Calls Are Positive

Knowing the obstacles that may trip you up and consciously choosing to overcome them are critical to living life successfully. Obstacles or problems can give you valuable clues. They are subtle invitations to explore your path further and work through the rough spots. Although they may seem negative, they are actually giving us an opportunity to grow and learn.

Some of the negative wake-up calls are listed below. Although we may be experiencing a negative situation, a wake-up call is positive if we choose to pay attention and correct it.

- ■ **Believing in luck.** If you and I believe someone is lucky then living a happy life is a matter of chance. Therefore, since there's nothing you can do why not just wait and hope things get better. This is *victim* thinking and gives us an excuse to whine or live life passively.

- ■ **Blaming others.** If you find yourself blaming your parents, boss, husband, children or friends, you are not accepting responsibility. Because we have free choice to change our situations, no one is trapped.

- ■ **If-only syndrome.** Every time you say "if only," you're really saying I don't believe this can happen and it's too late. "If only I had a better education." "If only I had the perfect wife or husband." "If only I made more money." What this means is you don't expect it to happen. Instead, say, "when I." For example, "When I earn more money, I will...." "When I meet my ideal partner, I will...."

■ **Over-scheduling.** By keeping yourself over-booked, you're ensuring you don't have the time to nurture yourself or build the quality relationships essential to happiness.

■ **Toxic friends.** If you find yourself surrounded with people who are stuck, negative, and have no desire to improve their situation, watch out. It may be time to assert yourself and let them know you are only interested in positive support for moving forward. Also, seek out people who inspire you, believe in you, and are self-motivated to improve and change.

■ **Afraid to be alone.** You are your best friend. Therefore, if it feels scary or uncomfortable to be alone, this is a "wake-up call" that something is wrong. A craving for constant stimulation is also a possible sign of fear.

For example, many years ago I dated a fun guy who loved to socialize with small groups of people. Now don't get me wrong, I love people too, but it became obvious he was always surrounded by friends. He hardly ever had time to himself and we were rarely alone. One evening he called for a date the coming weekend. I suggested we stay home and make a quiet dinner together. "That sounds great," he said.

Well, that Saturday evening I walked in his place and found two of his pals in the kitchen starting our dinner. Plus, he said, one of their new girlfriends was going to join us. I was disappointed we were not going to have time alone and told him how I felt. All he could say was, "Oh, we'll have a great time. We can always be alone another time." This was a person who needed an audience and constant attention and activity.

■ **Repetitive setbacks.** If you have a pattern of experiencing the same disappointments or challenges over and over this is a big wake-up call to check out why. These can include frequent job terminations, failed relationships, violent outbursts, and many more.

Years ago I met Paul, a personable, bright, mid-level manager who was never satisfied with his jobs because he had problems with his bosses. He complained they were unfair and had poor management skills and a variety of other personality or work style habits. As a result, he was always ready to leave and look for something better. When he finally realized these were powerful wake-up calls, things began to turn around.

After getting some feedback from past employers and current coworkers, he admitted he had a tough time communicating. Rather than deal honestly with his frustrations and discuss them in a healthy manner with his employers, Paul stuffed it. Since his bosses didn't have a clue anything was bothering him, how could they even begin to address it? It was easier for him to always "blame the boss" rather than taking personal responsibility for the working relationship. Paul now has a great job in a company and has learned to deal head on with his frustrations by communicating more openly. His pattern of failed working relationships is history.

Take Responsibility and Look Inside

For example, after many disappointing and failed relationships, I began to ask myself difficult questions. "Barbara, is it possible that you are unconsciously sabotaging your relationships and attracting emotionally unavailable men?" Sometimes it felt like I was wearing a sign that said, "Wanted: Men Unwilling and Unable to Make a Commitment." After a series of disappointing relationships, I had to admit, yes, it's possible I'm part of the problem. It was too easy to say, "All men are jerks." The signs were clearly pointing me in a direction to seek guidance.

I was strongly committed to taking a deep look at myself and began working with an incredible counselor. What an experience that was. I discovered that my independent nature, desire to control, and unwillingness to ask for help were not helping my cause. Because of my lack of vulnerability, some men felt I didn't need them. How could they do anything for a woman who appeared to be so competent? I learned I was also afraid to lose myself and my identity in a relationship. All of my fears were exposed and I began to make progress in dealing with my issues.

It would have been much easier to say, "There are no good men out there." Instead, I chose to work on myself and take action. About a year later I met my wonderful husband, Bob. This entire experience was a major breakthrough and an incredible opportunity to grow personally.

If you are in a marriage, dating, or work relationship that is stressful or upsetting, ask yourself, "Is this something I've experienced before?" Is there a possibility I am contributing to this disharmony. Every relationship has something to teach us and many are wake-up calls, as well. We will only grow if we are willing to look at our own weaknesses.

I'll admit if you are a busy, in-control, on-the-treadmill type of person, you may be afraid to admit weaknesses or seek help. Heaven knows, I was, until I realized it takes an incredible amount of strength and enlightenment to look within. I urge you to take a long, honest look at your life and pay attention to your wake-up calls.

Wake-up calls also come in positive forms, such as friends or coworkers who have the courage to tell you the truth. Many years ago, a dear friend of mine pointed out that my desire to be in control was impacting how we related to one another. At times, she felt I was insensitive to her needs. This came as a complete shock to me. However, I was grateful for her feedback. She obviously cared enough about me and our friendship to risk exposing her feelings. I took her comments to heart and did some serious soul-searching. As a result, I made a real effort to work on my weaknesses. Remember, wake-up calls come to us in many ways. The key is to notice them and take action.

Summary of Key Points

■ Be aware of obstacles that are sabotaging your success and happiness.

■ Identify any wake-up calls you may currently be receiving.

■ Learn to recognize the clues, invitations and guiding signs.

■ Begin eliminating or acting on your wake-up calls.

Exercise: Five-Minute Joy Booster

It's time to introduce you to a powerful exercise called the daily joy booster. Years ago, I realized that as soon as I woke up in the morning my mind was filled with stressful thoughts and negative chatter about deadlines and to-do lists. It occurred to me that if I filled my mind with joyful and pleasant thoughts and pictures of my dreams, I'd set the tone for the day. So I purposely put some inspirational books, quotes, and spiritual materials on my night stand.

From that day until now, I take five minutes for myself. Each morning as soon as I'm awake I prop up the pillows and read something inspirational for a minute or two. I allow the words to sink in and imagine myself totally blessed and happy. Then for another few minutes I create pictures of future dreams. Once I saw Bob and myself on a tropical vacation in a big hammock under a palm tree. I end my five minutes by expressing thanks for all I do have, ask for guidance, and say a little prayer. These precious five minutes give me such incredible joy and confidence and prepare me to weather the day's challenges. I call this proven, delightful process my joy booster.

At the end of each section, I will remind you to make the joy booster part of your daily routine. Every morning this week before you get out of bed, prop up the pillows, sit back, and take a few minutes to imagine one of your dreams. Then either say a little prayer, an affirmation, or read one of the quotes at the end of this section.

Exercise: The Color Clue Game

Sit in a comfortable, quiet, peaceful area. Purposely focus on a problem area or one of the signs you've been experiencing—perhaps pent-up anger, a series of failed relationships, the inability to relax and enjoy life, mounting debts, or whatever it is for you. Now, close your eyes and ask for guidance from the Lord, your spiritual source, or yourself, as follows: "What color best demonstrates how I'm feeling and how I should proceed?" Allow yourself to see any emerging color.

Red may mean you should stop and take no action at this time. Green likely suggests you take action and move forward. Yellow means proceed with caution or wait patiently for more guidance.

Be patient. If you are not used to going within to get answers you may have to try several times before you see a color. If no answer comes at that time, relax and let it go. Chances are you'll get a sudden inspirational thought within the next week or two.

Exercise: How Do I Feel?

In your Dream Big workbook, date a new page and at the top write, Guiding Signs and Obstacles—How Do I Feel? Now, on the left side of the page jot down as many obstacles, disappointments, or signs you can think of that are preventing you from your dream. Leave some space after each one to jot down how you *feel* about it on the right. For example:

Signs/Obstacles	My Feelings
I've been fired twice from a job.	I feel unappreciated and uncertain about my abilities.
I say "if only" a lot.	I feel like a victim and have no hope.
I blame others for my mistakes or inability to perform.	I feel angry often.

Now look at your list. You are certainly entitled to your feelings; however, they may not serve you well. Chances are, if you honestly deal with your feelings, seek support, and admit any flaws, you'll free yourself to move forward.

Dream Big Group Members or Partner

Share your guiding signs and feelings and ask for support.

Message for the Spiritually Inclined

It's important to know you are not alone as you embark on your journey. If you feel any apprehension, fear, or sense of being overwhelmed, repeat the following words, as needed. Again, insert your own term for your spiritual source.

Dear Lord, or _____, You are my eternal life and comfort. In the quietness of my soul, I can turn to God or _____ for any strength or reassurance I may need. As I listen, God speaks to me in a language my mind and heart can hear: "Walk with Me, My child, and draw upon My strength. The path you follow is one that I have created, so you need not fear what lies ahead. I will be with you, and I will lead you to a place of quiet solitude where you will find the comfort you seek."

—Excerpted from the *Daily Word*

■ ■ ■

Whatever you are going through, know that I am with you. I am there for you whether you think you need Me or not. You will never need to go through anything alone. Listen, for I will be there, encouraging you every moment of the day or night.

■ ■ ■

I will comfort you. (Isaiah 66:13)

Now ask for your own guidance:

Dear _____, Please give me the insight, strength, and guidance I need to clear up my issue/ problem with _____.

Week Two
Step 2: Listen to Your Heart–
Say "No" to Ms. Misery

*Most of us have been trained to automatically deny,
ignore or discount our intuitive feelings to the point
where we don't even know we have them. So we
need to retrain ourselves to recognize and pay
attention to our inner promptings.*
—Shakti Gawain, *The Path of Transformation*

I have good news and bad news. The good news is, you and I have a wonderful friend who guides us daily— our heart's desire or intuition. I named mine "Sparkles"—she thinks I can do anything and is the "wind beneath my wings." Unfortunately, most of us don't listen to our friend who is always trying to get our attention and knows exactly what we need to be happy. Why?

Because the bad news is, we all have an inner critic who enjoys seeing us worry and wants to make sure we never change a thing in our life. I named my critic "Ms. Misery." I imagine her sitting on my shoulder with a long black cape, pointed hat, warts all over her face, and long nose, constantly telling me what I can't do.

By naming my two voices and giving them identities, I found it allowed me to more effectively listen to divine guidance and ignore false fears. When you distinguish between your two voices, you can participate and play the game of life joyfully and effortlessly. Most of us rationalize, reason, and try to logically figure things out. We dismiss our hunches and gut feelings as frivolous dreams.

Yet to awaken your power and passion it's important to follow your hunches and let your heart or intuition be your guide. In Step 1, you identified wake-up calls to alert you to obstacles. In Step 2, you'll discover your own personal guide and learn how to tap into a powerful source of guidance available to you. I'm sure you've had gut feelings from time to time in which you feel like calling a friend, imagine owning your own business, moving to another city, or something similar. The key is to trust and act on these intuitive feelings without hesitation.

Follow Your Hunches

Let me share the story of Rick.

Rick is a top real estate agent. One busy day as he was sitting in his office, he had an unusual urge to go out and take a drive. No particular destination came to mind, but a little inner voice said, "Just go drive." Even though Rick was swamped with work and calls to return, he got in his car and began aimlessly driving around. He drove to a subdivision and ran into one of his past clients. After catching up on family and friends, the client said, "Rick, I'm selling my home and would like you to come by later this week and take my listing." Without any effort, Rick got a sale.

How many of us, doubting our hunch, would have said, "That's ridiculous. I can't go out for a drive now. I've got too much work to do." Skeptics will say, Rick was just lucky. Yet Rick was wise enough to follow his inner voice without question. In fact, Rick shared with me that he feels his "intuitive" hunches contribute greatly to his sales success. Imagine being a salesperson swamped with leads, yet always being guided to the prospects likely to buy each day. Wow—talk about targeting your selling efforts. Yes, it can and does happen. Bob and I also practice "intuitive" selling and it works. I can assure you, what appears to be luck is intuition and divine guidance in action.

Stop Efforting—Start Trusting

Whenever you rationalize, reason, and try to logically figure things out you are making an effort, or *efforting,* as we call it. However, when you trust your intuition and follow your hunches—life becomes easier and less stressful. In other words, you have to stop asking "how?" "But how am I going to create my ideal job?" "How am I going to be able to afford a month-long trip to Europe?" You are not supposed to figure it out or worry about "how." Your job is easy—just imagine the best, wait for a lead from your intuition, and act on it. Does this sound incredulous to you? Actually, it is quite simple. Still skeptical? Let's hear about Elaine Speece.

Many years ago I gave a keynote address called *Passion, Power and Prosperity: Put More in Your Life!* for the American Association of Medical Transcriptionists. In this powerful program I asked everyone to imagine what they would be doing if there were no obstacles, money was not an issue, and they were guaranteed success. We also made believe it was five years into the future and we had all achieved our dreams. It was amazing to feel the energy and excitement in the room as everyone shared their wonderful life with a neighbor.

One of the attendees, Elaine, was inspired to move toward her dream. She contacted me recently to give me an update on how my talk had impacted her.

Elaine Speece, CMT, of San Antonio, Texas, was getting hunches from her heart for years about opening her own business. In the early 1980s she was a Certified Medical Transcriptionist in a hospital. Because of the heavy workload some of the transcription was sent to an outside service. Elaine often felt the work was not up to her standards and said, "This is terrible work. I know I can do better."

She began getting little messages from her heart, "Elaine, if you can produce such excellent work in the hospital, you can do it for your own clients." This friendly voice sounded assured, solid, and supportive. Her fearful voice quickly fought back with, "You don't know anything about running a business, hiring staff, and paying taxes. There are other transcription services that are struggling right now. You don't know anything about all the new modern equipment. Are you crazy?" Fortunately, she listened to her heart. Shortly thereafter, a few doctors asked her to transcribe some tapes at home and her business was born.

In 1989 she got a five-thousand-dollar small business loan from her bank and began out of a spare bedroom in her home. Soon, she had one employee helping her and quickly added three more. Next, it was six stations in her converted garage. Finally she moved into office space and ended up with twenty-three employees. Elaine was featured in the September 1995 issue of *Entrepreneur* magazine. Elaine's successful business was born out of her early hunches.

Be Open to Divine Direction

In fact, all great things start with those little "seeds" and "ideas" we all get from our heart. You see, I really believe every time we get those exciting ideas it is God or our divine source giving us direction. The challenge is to keep the seed alive. I asked Elaine how she kept her dream alive and well during the early years. She said, "I just asked for guidance every step of the way. I would say, 'Lord, if it is time for me to get office space, please let me know. I'm interviewing right now—please help me select the perfect employee who will be loyal and an asset to my business.' I just prayed each day and asked for guidance."

I asked Elaine how she knew her prayers were being answered or she was receiving the guidance she needed. She said, "When I had to make a decision, if it was right I always had a good, positive feeling. If it didn't feel right or became a struggle, I just didn't act."

Elaine also mentioned she read a quote one day when she was starting her business and felt it was a special sign for her to follow her dream. "For I know the plans I have for you," says the Lord. "They are plans for good and not for disaster, to give you a future and a hope" (Jeremiah 29:11). Over the years she has found that scripture to be the foundation for building her business.

We have to get used to the idea of checking in or consulting with ourselves for answers. Most of us look for guidance externally—we ask friends, read books, and attend seminars. Although these resources may be helpful, everything we need to know is within us.

Take Action

Next, we have to have the courage and faith to act on our intuition. For most of us, this is the most difficult and scary part. Acting on your intuition when you don't know how or why is like walking down a flight of stairs blindfolded, trusting you'll get to the bottom safely. Following our hunches means taking action or making changes. Rick, the realtor, had to physically get into his car and drive around. He took *action*. Elaine went to get a small business loan. She took *action*.

You may be thinking, "But how do I know if it's my *intuition* and not my fearful mind?" The key is to notice *how* the voice is speaking to you. If your inner voice sounds fearful, guilty, afraid, or worried, it's not your intuition. Typically, whether your intuition is giving you happy, serious, or sad information, it feels right, clear, matter-of-fact. A strong word of caution. Whenever you hear your mind say "you should," "you can't," or "What if _____ happens?" don't listen. Fight back immediately. "Don't you dare try to scare me." It can take years of practice before you even realize you have two voices. Believe me, you do. We all do.

Many people find it helpful to give their inner voices names. My nagging, fearful voice, Ms. Misery, is a hideous creature who sounds and looks like a witch. Whenever I get excited about a new dream or goal, she immediately discourages and scares me in her shrill, whiny voice. Sparkles, my intuition, is enthusiastic and supportive and encourages me to *think big*.

In 1987, I was relaxing one day on my sofa when I heard Sparkles say, "Barbara, wouldn't you like to speak in an exotic place?" I thought, yes—but where? At this point, most of my traveling was to U.S. cities. "How about South America?" Sparkles asked. I thought that was a great idea. Images of Rio de Janeiro popped up in my head and the words to the song, "Girl From Ipanema" played in my mind. Now I was really getting excited!

In a flash, Ms. Misery arrived on the scene. In a shrill, witch-like voice she said, "You think you can just go speak in South America? Ha! You don't speak Spanish, you have no contacts in South America. That's a ridiculous idea." For a minute I must admit, I thought it was pretty crazy. It's true. I don't speak any Spanish. I don't know a soul in South America. What do I have worth saying that companies would fly me all the way to South America for? Suddenly, I realized I was falling in the trap of believing Ms. Misery was giving me sound advice. My dream was waning. I got angry and said, "Buzz off, Ms. Misery. I'm going to South America." All I did was imagine it and tuck it away as a future dream. I took absolutely no action whatsoever.

Several months after that incident, I got a call from Bill Anderson, an association executive who had hired me the year before to speak at his convention in Phoenix. Bill said, "Barbara, one of the delegates who heard you in Phoenix is hosting a conference this June in Buenos Aires, Argentina. He would like you to be the keynote speaker on quality service based on your book. In addition, we will give you two round-trip tickets so you can take a guest. Can you do it?" At this point I had goose bumps from head to toe, but I calmly said, "Hold on, Bill, let me check my calendar." I put him on hold and proceeded to scream and dance like a madwoman for about twenty seconds. I got back on the phone and calmly told Bill the dates were available.

As soon as I was done with Bill, I quickly called my friend, Cynthia. When she answered, I excitedly told her I had been asked to speak in Buenos Aires that June and an international association had given me two round-trip tickets. "Who are you going to take? Your mother? Your sister?" Cynthia asked. At that time in my life, I wasn't dating a soul and there was no one on the horizon. However, I was longing to meet my ideal mate and be in a loving, committed relationship. Once again Sparkles inspired me. It seemed so unbelievable, but I heard myself say, "No, Cynthia, I'm not going to take my mother or my sister. I'm going to go to South America with the man of my dreams who I'll most likely end up marrying." To this day, I cannot believe the words came out of my mouth.

Two months later I went to dinner with Cynthia at MacArthur Park, a popular San Francisco restaurant. That night I met a wonderful man, Bob Romano, and we started a close relationship. Six months later we both flew off to Buenos Aires where I spoke at the conference and played with Bob for a fantastic week. We then went to Rio de Janeiro and toured Brazil for another fabulous and romantic three weeks. Two weeks after our return home Bob proposed to me. We have been happily married for ten years.

It seems like magic that two of my fantasy dreams occurred so easily, so effortlessly. The South America trip occurred because I spent a lot of time marketing to associations and imagined one day I'd get a speaking engagement in Buenos Aires or Rio. My relationship with Bob appeared after a string of disappointments. However, I never gave up and clearly saw myself in a fulfilling relationship. I learned a powerful lesson from this experience. If I can imagine it and believe it, I can have it! If you can imagine it and believe it, you can have it!

To Which Voice Do You Listen?

How often do you dismiss your wild thoughts as simply foolish or unrealistic? Maybe you want to open your own business, travel to an exotic location, or live in a dream home. If you're a sales professional, you'd like to be number one worldwide, break every record ever made, and earn a trip to Hawaii. Perhaps you long to simplify your life, spend more time with your family, take a job with less money, and move to a rural area. To which voice do you listen? If you dream it, you can have it.

Are you guilty of not dreaming big enough? As a spiritual person I believe our intuition is direct inspiration and guidance from above. All you have to do is Dream Big. Then listen very carefully to your intuition. At this point, do not be concerned with "how." Dare to dream and Dream Big.

What about you? What has your little voice been telling you to act on? It may be something fun—taking a trip, moving to an exciting destination. It may be something scary. Starting your own business. Deciding to start a family. It may even be something painful. Ending a relationship or getting some help for some personal problems you've been denying.

One thing about your intuition. It is relentless and will not give up on you easily. Your inner voice or God, loves you very much. Even if you try to push it aside and ignore it, it will keep popping up again and again trying to get your attention. And for good reason. I believe your intuition is a guiding light, a messenger sent to point you in the right direction. When you ignore your intuition, you're choosing a life of struggle, worry, and fear. When you listen to your intuition, you are going with the natural flow of life.

Now it's time for you to get to work. Ask yourself, "What has my intuition or God been trying to tell me? Quit my job? Take a long vacation? Work on a relationship?"

Summary of Key Points
■ Distinguish between your two inner voices and name them.

■ Conquer fear and doubt.

- Receive the clear guidance you need to use the make it happen process effectively.
- Listen and act on your divine guidance.

Exercise: Five-Minute Joy Booster

Every morning this week before you get out of bed, prop up the pillows, sit back, and take a few minutes to imagine one of your dreams. Then either say a little prayer, an affirmation, or read one of the quotes at the end of this section.

Note: If you are having trouble doing this exercise or resisting it, ask yourself why. Do you doubt you can have your dream? Does it make you uncomfortable? Why are you unwilling to give yourself five precious minutes to invest in your future? If your mind wanders, be kind to yourself—it's normal. I still struggle with this myself. Just allow yourself to enjoy this five minutes of precious time to go within. Start with three minutes, if necessary.

Exercise: Voices in the Chairs

Take two chairs and imagine one is your loving, excited heart who wants you to be happy. Choose a name such as "Wise One" or "Rainbow." If you can't think of a name, begin the exercise anyway. When you're done, see if a name comes to you.

My heart is called _____.

Now imagine the other chair is your fearful, negative voice. Choose a name for this side of you such as "Grumpy," "Scaredy Cat," or "Party Pooper."

My fearful voice is called _____.

Put your book down and sit in your "heart" chair. Start a conversation out loud and imagine you are sharing your hopes and dreams with your fearful voice. Be as excited, hopeful, and positive as you possibly can. For example, you may enthusiastically say, "I decided I'm going to start my own catering business. I'm going to be very successful. Then I'm going to go on a fun trip to Italy." I know you may feel foolish, but trust me—this is a very powerful exercise.

As soon as you finish expressing your thoughts, move to your fear chair and let your fearful voice try to totally discourage you. "Have you lost your mind? You have a great job with benefits." Now go back to your heart chair and in your most convincing voice assure your fearful voice you will be fine and are indeed going to pursue your dreams. Keep switching between chairs until all parties have come to an agreement. Now quickly, while it's fresh in your mind, take out your Dream Big workbook and write down all the thoughts, hopes and dreams expressed by both your heart and fearful voice.

On the top of a new page write, "My heart,_____ _____, totally believes in me and feels that I need to: (write everything that comes to mind and don't worry about how you will accomplish these goals)."

On a new page write, "My fearful voice, _____ _____, is afraid the following will happen: (list all your fears)."

Look carefully at the two discussions. I'm sure your fearful voice was not exactly encouraging. What can you do to build your voice's confidence? Notice the direction and guidance your heart is giving you. This is the truth, your future—you must accept it as a gift and an opportunity. Now for some good news. What if I told you that your heart is *divine guidance* or *God* talking to you? What would you say? Would you dare not listen? Let that be a vote of confidence to *go for it!*

Note: Feel free to do the "two voices" exercise with a partner if your prefer. You may feel more comfortable if you are supported by someone you trust.

Dream Big Group Members or Partner

Share your name for your heart and fearful voice. Also share what you wrote down in your workbook exercise.

Message for the Spiritually Inclined

Make sure you are awake each day ready to receive direction and guidance. Try these affirmations and prayers to ask for direction and then listen carefully for leads in the following weeks and months.

Dear Lord or _____, Give me a definite lead, reveal to me my perfect self-expression, show me which talent I am to make use of now.

■ ■ ■

Dear Lord or _____, Open the way for the divine design of my life to manifest; let the genius within me now be released; let me see clearly the perfect plan: health, wealth, love, and perfect self-expression.
(Both of the above affirmations excerpted from Florence Schovel Shinn's, *The Game of Life and How to Play It.*)

■ ■ ■

God, wherever You guide me, I will follow.

■ ■ ■

Write your own request or prayer in your workbook.

Week Three
Step 3: Test the Waters—Take the Risk Out of Risk

I believe the greatest risk in life is one day we'll look back at a life full of regrets for unfulfilled dreams or mistaken priorities. Nothing scares me more than to think one day I might look back at my life and say, "I always wished I had taken that trip to Italy I dreamed of," "I always wished I had spent more time with my family and friends," "I always wished I had learned to play the guitar," and so forth.

In Step 2, you learned how to listen to your heart and trust your intuition. Now you must take action. Step 3 asks us to test the waters and take some risks. We've all heard that famous expression, "No risk—no reward." It's so true. Risk does require making changes. Yet so many of us go through life afraid to change a thing. We stay at the same job, even though we hate it. We eat at the same restaurants. We live in areas we don't enjoy. We may even stay in unhealthy relationships. That's not living. We're tiptoeing our way cautiously through life. Why would we choose to live this way? Because imaginary fears and walls immobilize us.

Step 3 offers practical tools to help you overcome your fears. Doubt and worry are useless emotions. By testing the waters you can take the risk out of risk. Fear is simply imagination out of control. Isn't that great news? Your fears are nothing more than imagined thoughts.

> *Fear is simply*
> *imagination out of control.*

Seek Support and Encouragement

When you discuss your fears with others, often you'll get the support and encouragement you need to get unstuck. Those closest to you can often see your potential before you can. I remember when I was thinking of leaving my full-time job to pursue a professional speaking career. As I shared my plans with my friends and business associates, most of them were quite encouraging. "Oh, you'll be great. I always knew you could do it. You're the entrepreneurial type." I thought, "I am? How come they believe in me and I'm scared?"

My own mother said, "Go for it." I remember saying, "Gee, Mom, aren't you going to tell me I already have a good-paying job with three weeks vacation, a company car, and benefits?" But she didn't try to talk me out of it. I thought, "I guess I have to go through with this." I was terrified. It's funny, but I used to think people who took risks in life had no fear. Otherwise, how could they possibly do such great things? I guess they're not afraid of failure. If I'm so afraid of making a mistake I probably don't have what it takes.

I began talking to other people who were self-employed speakers, trainers, and consultants. I asked, "How did you feel when you first went out on your own?" Every single one of them admitted they were filled with both apprehension and excitement. But something made them break right through the fear and pursue their dreams. This was so encouraging for me to hear. It's normal for us to feel the fear. The key is to not let it stop us.

Talk to others who share the same challenges and experiences. In my case I spoke to other people who were already in my profession. I even joined the National Speakers Association while I still worked at my job. By learning more about what others had done, their successes and failures, I felt more prepared to take a risk.

What's the Worst That Can Happen?

I thought, "What do I have to lose? What's the worst that can happen? If it doesn't work out I'll go back and get a job." And then it hit me. The worst that can happen is one day I'll regret never pursuing my full potential. I'd rather give it all I've got, and if it doesn't work out at least I can always look myself in the mirror and say, "I did my best."

My mother amazed me with her spunk and courage late in life. After my dad and grandmother passed away, my mom was living alone in New Jersey near some relatives. My sister, Patricia, and I were both in different cities on the West Coast. We asked her if she'd consider moving to San Francisco so we could be closer. The usual concerns came up—moving such a long distance, packing up a big house, and starting over in a strange city. However, overall, she was genuinely open to the idea and actually seemed a bit excited.

At the time, she was fifty-eight and said, "By my sixtieth birthday I'll move to San Francisco." In the next months, she began moving toward her dream and working through her fear. By packing up boxes, holding a garage sale, and preparing for her imminent move, it became more real and less scary.

When she turned sixty, she left her familiar neighborhood and relatives, and moved to San Francisco. Slowly but surely, she got involved in senior citizens and church activities where she made friends and began going on trips. Now she is on the board of several groups. The funny thing is, prior to that she had never belonged to any groups or volunteered her time. Her self-esteem, confidence, and happiness have soared since her life-changing move to San Francisco.

Beware of Naysayers

Earlier you met Katie, who created the wonderful job at the winery. She has some words of wisdom about risk:

> Risk is scary sometimes because you feel you are stepping into the unknown; however, risk will only bring you closer to your dream. If one avenue doesn't work; try another. It then becomes a process of elimination. Don't quit after just one try or allow others to sabotage your efforts. Sometimes when friends or family members learn of your take-action posture, they feel threatened. They unintentionally may want you to feel crappy about your life, because they feel crappy about their life and they want company!! It's not a nice thing to say about people but it's sometimes true.
>
> I had a bookkeeping business for about two years and was just getting on my feet. My office was in my home and my husband was making a lot more money than I was, so I had the luxury of not stressing too much about finances. Then my relationship with my husband was on the outs, and I eventually decided to leave. I still wanted

to run my business especially since it allowed me a lot of freedom, but I was terrified that I might not be able to make financial ends meet.

I decided that my emotional sanity was more important and if I needed to find a position as an employee somewhere, so be it. I decided to risk it. I found a small studio apartment; moved in, and was very low on cash. The phone started ringing in about a month. Potential new clients called asking if I was available to do their small business bookkeeping. Within six months I was making more money than I had before. It was a risk to take, but it paid off in more ways than one.

Be Willing to Let Go

Sometimes taking risks can involve "letting go" of situations or people to whom we have grown attached. At twenty-six years old, Padi, a friend of mine, opened her own advertising and public relations firm with one employee. Fifteen years later with 15 employees, her company was the largest agency in Northern California, handling clients such as Hewlett-Packard and the *New York Times*. In addition to financial success, she had her own TV show, a newspaper column, and a gorgeous office, and was well respected in her market and community. Padi admitted, "My ego received lots of self-gratification and I was hooked on success."

As often is the case, very little in life stays the same. In the last two years of her business, Padi began to experience a series of difficult challenges. Her best friend, Angela, and key Vice President in her business, suddenly announced she was leaving the business in two weeks to write "The Great American Novel." Padi hadn't a clue this was coming and was devastated, hurt, and surprised. Angela was a friend Padi trusted, socialized with, and loved like a sister. To make matters worse she would not give Padi a reason and just kept saying, "I can't talk about it." Padi was so concerned she had caused the problem, she offered to go to counseling with Angela.

Three weeks after Angela left, Padi found out she had opened her own firm and taken some key staff members and clients. Shortly after that, Padi's father suffered a massive heart attack and she flew to the East Coast to be with her family while he recuperated. By now her billings were going down and finances became tight. As work became a struggle, Padi felt depressed and began to lose her drive. Somehow she managed to keep things together and stabilized her business. However, she no longer was happy with her work and began to hate the business.

Afraid people might think she failed if she shut the doors, she kept hanging on. She contemplated, "What am I going to do now? I've spent all these years building this business—I can't just let go." Fear consumed her as she imagined the worst. She actually fantasized how the subject of her failure would become lunchtime gossip around town, and she would become humiliated and no longer the respected local business woman. Finally, she realized she had to let go as her emotional and physical well-being were impacted. After much torment, Padi sold her company and started a totally new and successful career as a professional speaker. I'm happy to say she is a peer and a dear friend.

Get Closer to the Fear

Right now you have hopes and desires. Your heart is speaking to you about unfulfilled dreams you must act on or actions you need to take to get on with your life. You're probably a little bit nervous. Perhaps you want to leave your job, buy a house, end a relationship, or move to a new city. Whatever it is requires taking a risk. To take the risk out of risk—move toward it.

If you always wanted to move to Colorado, write to the Visitors and Conventions Bureau and get some literature. Rent some videos on Colorado. Talk to other people who moved to other cities. Share your dream with your friends. It is possible to work through fear by immersing yourself in it.

In the Introduction I talked about my support group of friends. We met about every four to six weeks and shared our dreams. The best part was admitting our fears and giving words of encouragement to one another.

I had the pleasure of addressing my fellow speakers at a chapter meeting some time ago. Marilyn Schott, a seminar leader and speaker, was inspired to Dream Big after my program. She told me for years she too met with a group of friends who came together to support one another to reach their dreams. (You'll read more about Marilyn and her friends later on.) By rooting for each other they didn't let themselves give up when the going got tough. And believe me, the going will get tough. The key is to prepare for it.

If you are really serious about creating your future, invite others to share your dreams. Find people who are open-minded, positive, good role models. Beware of those who mean well but are threatened by your plans. You know the type. They are always ready with a "what if" or "you should" comment. Think about this. If you have the guts and the energy to pursue your dreams, what about them? They know that if you can do it, what's their excuse? They don't have any. You force them to come face-to-face with their inability to fully embrace their own life.

Sometimes our own spouse, partner, best friend, children, and coworkers will try to "guide us" back to our senses. They want to prevent us from making some terrible mistake. It's important not to get sidetracked from your plan, especially if your "heart" or divine guidance is talking to you. Take in their unsolicited "advice," check out your options, and then do what is right for you. No one has the right to rob us of achieving what is destined for us, our divine plan.

Create a Dream Big Group

If you haven't formed your own Dream Big support group by now, do it. Or at least get a dream partner. When you work with a group of people who all have hopes, dreams, fears, and a desire to make a difference—it's extremely rewarding. In fact, Jesus Christ said, "If two of you shall agree on earth as touching anything that they shall ask, it shall be done for them of my Father which is in Heaven." (See the Invitation to Join the Big Dream Club in the back of the book.)

Summary of Key Points

■ Identify your own fears and doubts.

■ Work through a specific area where you feel afraid to take a risk.

■ Test the waters by taking an action step to take the risk out of risk.

Exercise: Five-Minute Joy Booster

Every morning this week before you get out of bed, prop up the pillows, sit back, and take a few minutes to imagine one of your dreams. Then either say a little prayer, an affirmation, or read one of the quotes at the end of this section. Note: If you haven't guessed by now, I obviously feel strongly about the importance of starting each day with your joy booster. Keep up the good work. If you forget now and then, don't worry about it.

Exercise: What's the Worst That Can Happen?

In your Dream Big workbook, note the date and jot down on a new page, What's the Worst That Can Happen? Now look back in your notebook at what you jotted down under the Voices in the Chair exercise from the second week. If you acted on your heart's guidance or your intuition and it didn't work out, what's the worst that could happen? Write it down. Typically, you'll find that our worst fears are either highly exaggerated or something we can deal with. Remember, the greatest fear of all can be a life filled with regrets. Don't let that happen to you.

Dream Big Group Members or Partner

Share a few fears from your workbook and ask the group, "What's the worst that can happen?" for encouragement on taking a risk.

Message for the Spiritually Inclined

Don't let imagined fears or doubts stop you from taking risks or making desired changes in your life. Support is readily available—you are not alone. For encouragement, read the following words as often as necessary:

As I let go and let God,
new opportunities open to me.

■ ■ ■

No matter how many plans I make or how much I prepare for some event, nothing much will come of it unless I take action. So I make today a day for acting on my beliefs, a day for stepping out in faith, a day for knocking on the door to new and greater opportunities!

■ ■ ■

"Knock and the door will be opened." (Luke 11:9)

■ ■ ■

God or _____ is working wonders and the best is yet to be. What possibilities does the future hold for us? We don't know for certain, but what we do know is that with God or _____ in charge, the only limitations on our possibilities come from our own imagination. We look beyond what seems to be reality and behold the possibilities of God's or _____ splendor at work! Yes, the best is yet to be!

■ ■ ■

"For mortals it is impossible, but not for God; for God all things are possible." (Mark 10:27)

Week Four
Step 4: Effort Less—
Enjoy the Ride

As one door shuts, another door opens

I bless the past, and forget it.
I bless the future knowing it has in store for me
endless joys. I live fully in the now.
—Florence Scovel Shinn

Many of us love control. We know what we want, when we want it, how we want it—and that we want it yesterday. However, when we try to control events or people in our lives, we become exhausted. Once we understand that control is an illusion, life gets easier. Can you imagine planting a seed, watering it and checking it daily for growth. We'd be totally frustrated and impatient. The seed will sprout when it's ready and not before. Likewise, think of your thoughts as little seeds or prayers that will get results at the right time. You can't control the timing or the result.

Step 4 asks that we *effort less* and helps you learn to *expect the best* without being attached to the outcome. Easier said than done. The lesson for us to learn is to relax and trust that all is well. Energy spent on worrying is precious time wasted. In week four you'll learn how to effort less and enjoy life more in preparation for your dream to happen. After all, the only thing we can control are our own thoughts and words. And therein lies our true power.

Control has many downsides: It causes burnout, limits ideas, and robs us of the joy of being surprised. How can we be surprised when we know exactly what to expect? The secret to "making" it happen is "letting" it happen. Sound like a contradiction? It's effortless.

Let It Happen

It's important to do the work. If you trust the process and have faith, you can confidently expect results. Instead of passively waiting for guidance, prepare and choose your dreams, actively wait with expectation and then seize the opportunity. When you try to *make it happen* and forget to *let it happen*, you are efforting and controlling the outcome.

Your job is to first Dream Big, put your order in to God or your spiritual source, wait for guidance, take action, then let go and get out of the way. Rest assured you will get additional signs and direction. I call these "divine inspiration." Ask and expect to get answers. If it feels like a struggle or an effort, however, back off and give yourself some time until it feels right.

Many years ago, I worked for a company in a staff position with significant responsibilities. Although I enjoyed my job, I wanted to stay with the company and move to another area. At the time, sales and marketing was becoming a big focus due to the competitive environment. In spite of the fact I had no previous sales experience, I wanted to be involved in selling the company's services. For at least six months, I doggedly pursued a position as a sales rep with a new product line. It all came down to a final interview between me and one other women. Excitement consumed me as I imagined finally realizing my dream job. I was devastated when I didn't receive a job offer.

Physical exhaustion set in and a touch of depression from all my hard efforts. After about two weeks of feeling sorry for myself, Sparkles, my intuition, said, "Barbara, relax, something better is coming along." Believing that my intuition was actually "divine inspiration," I immediately felt a sense of calmness.

About a month later, I decided to try to create a new sales position in the company and approached a senior executive with my ideas. Much to my delight, he offered me a job on the spot. As a result of good training, divine inspiration and persistence on my part, I excelled in sales and made the President's Club. Later I became a regional sales manager.

Oh, by the way, shortly after I created my new sales position, I found out the job I originally wanted was eliminated and the entire division closed down. The lesson I learned was, if it feels like a battle to get something done, or it's just not working, expect something better.

I remember I was afraid to leave my job and start my business until I had some speaking dates lined up. Working for a seminar company sounded like a great idea to me. Since they guarantee a minimum number of dates each month I figured I could survive until I developed my own business. For months I sent letters, made calls, and asked friends to put in a good word. It was not happening. I was devastated. How could I get this close to reaching my goal and hit a brick wall?

Ms. Misery, my fearful voice, really gave it to me. "See, Barbara, I told you it was a ridiculous idea. You better just stay at the bank and come back to your senses." Fortunately, Sparkles, my divine messenger said, "Barbara, did it ever occur to you that maybe you don't need to work for a seminar company? You are supposed to do this on your own. Show faith, quit your job, and trust that all is well." What a battle. I was so sure I could control the process, I didn't allow for any other options.

Ask for Guidance

After praying for guidance, I felt a strong desire to quit my job. Finally, I just gave up control, stopped worrying, and resigned in early December 1985. I was scared out of my wits and had very little business lined up. I was in discussion with a telecommunications company two weeks before I resigned, but there was no signed agreement. I was concerned about this and thought of keeping my job a bit longer.

Three days after I quit at the bank, the telecommunications company called and asked if I would do a series of twenty-four seminars over the next three months. In the first ninety days I made the equivalent of a whole year's salary at the bank. Efforting wasn't working for me: When I began to effort less and trust more, I let it happen naturally.

Stop Pushing—Let It Happen

Have you ever tried so hard to make something happen it was exhausting? Nothing seemed to work out. Perhaps you hoped to find a new job, close a big sale, or start a new venture. In the beginning it was fun and exciting. Energized and creative, your ideas flowed easily.

However, after hitting many brick walls and dead ends, frustration and worry set in. You push harder and harder to make things happen. Stop! Take a deep breath and assess the situation: "Whatever I'm doing is obviously not working. It shouldn't be this difficult. Let me back off, ask for guidance and give up control."

Be Spontaneous

Allowing for spontaneity in our lives is another way to practice "going with the flow." Unlike the previous examples that may involve months and years of struggle, being spontaneous is an easy "baby step" we can all take. I, too, struggle with being more spontaneous. But when I do let go, I am often pleasantly surprised at the outcome.

One evening I was determined to go to one of our favorite restaurants in San Diego. Bob said, "Let's just go out, drive around, and look for a new place to eat," I couldn't believe what I was hearing. Did he actually want to drive around aimlessly in the hope we'd find something we both liked? Going out without a specific destination in mind was a foreign concept to me.

Seeing the puzzled and fearful look on my face, he said, "Be a little adventurous, Barbara. This can be fun. Here's your chance to try to be more spontaneous."

Well, that did it. As uncomfortable as I was with the idea, I agreed. We drove around for a while and noticed a fun restaurant we had heard about recently. The parking lot was packed, which we took as a good sign. We walked in to check it out. The menu looked wonderful and the atmosphere was unique. Because of a last-minute cancellation, we got in after just fifteen minutes.

I learned an important lesson: The more spontaneous we are the more surprises life gives us.

Sometimes as parents we try to force our children to pursue certain careers or sports or to join activities they may not enjoy. As bosses we may try to control the work style of one of our associates. As spouses we may try to get our partners to change their behaviors. In all of these cases, we certainly can suggest ideas and offer helpful hints. However, it's important that we are not attached to the outcome and demand performance. In fact, in some cases we may have to literally "let go" of our expectations and take care of ourselves.

Let Go and Satisfy Yourself

My friend Padi, whom you met in a previous chapter, shared an interesting story with me.

> I love flowers and for years I tried to get my husband to bring them to me on a regular basis. I started with subtle hints, quickly moved on to asking, cajoling and finally gave up at the begging stage. Nothing seemed to work. I even left him reminder notes. He meant well, buying them on special occasions (which are only a few times a year, unfortunately) and forgetting about them the rest of the time. My disappointment made this otherwise wonderful and thoughtful man feel like a failure with me. Meanwhile, I was increasingly frustrated because I felt this was such a simple request.
>
> One day the light went on: If I wanted flowers so badly, why not send them to myself? That day, I placed a standing order with a local florist for two beautiful arrangements to be sent to my home every Friday. We each got what we wanted once I let go of wanting him to do something that didn't fit his personality. I got my flowers and he got me off his case.

Is there someone in your life now you are trying to change and control? It may be someone who works for you or with you, even your own boss. Or maybe it's your spouse, children, or a close friend. Is it possible there is a way to "ease up" on your expectations, let it go completely or just take care of it yourself, like Padi?

Even Christ advised us not to worry: "Your Heavenly Father already knows all your needs, and He will give you all your needs from day to day if you live for Him and make the Kingdom of God your primary concern. So don't worry about tomorrow, for tomorrow will bring it's own worries. Today's trouble is enough for today."

> *If I'm forcing something to happen,*
> *it isn't right for me.*

What are you trying to control in your life? Maybe it's time to let go, relax, and trust that all is well.

Summary of Key Points

■ Effort less and enjoy more.

■ Understand the secret to "making it happen" and "letting it happen"—you need to do both.

■ Avoid "pushing and forcing" events in your life.

■ Give up control and let go when appropriate.

Exercise: Five-Minute Joy Booster

Every morning this week before you get out of bed, prop up the pillows, sit back, and take a few minutes to imagine one of your dreams. Then either say a little prayer, an affirmation, or read one of the quotes at the end of this section.

Exercise: Effort Less and Give Up Control

On a new page in your Dream Big workbook, write Give Up Control at the top and date it. Think of all the people, areas, and situations in your life that are causing you frustration and you are trying to control. Jot them down quickly. Be sure to put the name or situation and what is bothering you. For example:

1. My boss always points out my mistakes and forgets to praise me. I wish I could change his management style.

2. My son won't clean up his room—I keep trying to force him with a lot of yelling and threats.

3. I've been passed over for a promotion the second time even though I got my MBA.

4. We still don't have the money for the down payment for a new house. I'm getting discouraged.

After you finish, reflect on your list. Could some of these be taken care of by having an honest, heart-to-heart talk with the person and asking for their suggestions on how to resolve it together? Is it time to try a new approach? Perhaps you could just say, "I need to let go of this situation and accept it as it is. This will work itself out in due time."

Life doesn't have to be a struggle—it can be easy and effortless when we stop trying and simply enjoy the ride. Giving up control and letting go is another key to living with passion and opening up possibilities.

Dream Big Group Members or Partner

Share some of your control issues and ask the group for ideas on how to let go.

Message for the Spiritually Inclined

The following words are powerful and comforting. If you are experiencing any struggle or fear, take a few minutes each day to read these words and know that all is well, despite outward appearances.

Let Go, Let God

I give thanks for the divine order that is governing every situation in my life. I am willing to let go and let God, because I know that each time I do, I am opening the door to endless possibilities.

■ ■ ■

Dear _____, I cast the burden within to you and know that all is well.

—Florence Shinn, Game of Life

■ ■ ■

When I stop trying to make something happen and just allow myself to be in partnership with God or _____ in letting it happen, I am amazed with the results. Obstacles to my goals disappear and doors to opportunities open to me.

—Excerpted from the *Daily Word*

■ ■ ■

"Can all your worries add a single moment to your life?" Of course not! (Luke 12:25)

■ ■ ■

"Don't worry about anything, pray about everything. Tell God what you need, and thank Him for all He has done. If you do this you will experience God's peace, which is far more wonderful than the human mind can understand."(Philippians 4:6,7)

■ ■ ■

Dear _____, Help me to let go of my struggle with _____. .

Step 5: Dream Big–Imagine the Best That Can Happen

Now comes the exciting part. You get to imagine your wildest dreams! Right now your dreams are sitting dormant waiting to be activated.

Unfortunately, as we grow up people tell us to be "realistic" and "consider ourselves lucky" for what we do have. As a result, our imagination muscles get flabby from lack of use. Most people define a dream as "a fantasy event in my life never meant to occur." My definition of a dream is "a future event in my life *waiting* to occur." Sound too good to be true? The key word is "waiting." It's up to you and me to make it happen and let it happen. Imagine—a future event in your life *waiting* to occur. This week you'll begin the powerful and exciting process of learning how to open up your mind to incredible possibilities.

> *A dream is a future event in my life waiting to occur.*

Most of us are guilty of dreaming too small. I assure you that no matter how much you dream, it's not big enough. Fear of failure, feelings of unworthiness, and lack of spiritual nourishment prevent us from attaining what we truly deserve to be happy, successful and fulfilled. Many businesses spend thousands of dollars each year on sales training to give their people skills to increase sales and customer satisfaction. It is typically not enough to motivate the sales representatives to want to succeed. We much teach people to see a direct connection between their work achievements and personal happiness.

I am not saying training is a waste of time, however. In fact, our company offers excellent sales, sales management, and customer service training. The key is to make sure we also give people the skills they need to create their future and honor their values.

A Dream Team Approach

Tim Schwartz is a Regional Sales Manager with Dionex, a leader in manufacturing research instrumentation. In August 1996 I presented a presentation at Dionex's national sales meeting called *Winning Sales Strategies of Top Performers*. I shared many ideas on positioning in the marketplace, being persistent, providing excellent service, concluding with my Dream Big message. At the end of my program, Tim thanked me and told me he was moved by my program. He also promised to call me when he created his dream.

At the time his region was not doing as well as he wanted. In my session, Tim wrote down, "The central region is now the number one region this year and I'm going to make President's Club with my sales reps." He checked with his reps who also heard my program and asked them to share their Dream Big goals. Nearly all had the same dream—to be the number one region.

Tim was determined not to let the dream die. Back at the office he encouraged his people to cut out pictures of things they wanted in their life. He knew meeting sales goals and making money is not as motivating as choosing *how* we will spend the money. One of his reps was renting but dreamed of owning a condo. He began collecting pictures of condos to add to his Dream Big board. Another rep wanted a cruise to Alaska. He kept his dream alive by cutting out pictures of cruise ships and making up a fake pay stub with an increased commission check.

A year later, I'll never forget the call I got from Tim. He excitedly announced, "Barbara, my region made number one and I'm off on the President's Club cruise. Thanks for your help."

Tim not only had a big dream for himself, he invited his team to share in his dream with powerful results for all. When we are focused on helping others, chances are our dreams will manifest quickly. I asked Tim, "What's your next dream?" He informed me that no region in the company has ever been number one for two years in a row and he's decided to go for it. All of his sales reps are up to the challenge and using the *making it happen* process to do it again.

Tim admitted that at times he struggled with feelings of unworthiness in asking to be number one. After all, there were homeless and starving people in the world and he could be focused on a more humanitarian goal. So he prayed for help and was handsomely rewarded for his faith and commitment to his people. I feel it is significant that although Tim was focused on achieving practical goals he still asked his spiritual source for guidance.

Help Is Readily Available

Often we try hard to make things happen and do it by ourselves. We forget that help is available simply by asking and believing our requests and prayers will be answered. What are you struggling with now? Relax and let go.

Although we may not have the opportunity to solve the worlds' problems, we can make a difference in our own way. By sharing the Dream Big philosophy we can get powerful results in motivating people at work, on a sales team or with our family members. Don't be afraid to reach out to those around you and encourage them to move toward their dreams. Let's not be so self-absorbed that we miss an opportunity to help a friend or associate in need of guidance.

Seeing Is Believing

Marilyn Schott, a seminar leader I mentioned earlier, approached me at a National Speaker's Convention and said, "I heard you speak last year and you gave us some ideas on how to Dream Big. It's working and you won't believe it." Apparently, Marilyn and three of her friends sat around her dining room table with piles of beautiful issues of *Architectural Digest, Town and Country,* and many other magazines. They had a ball ripping out all the pictures and words of things that they wanted. They each created a dream book filled with pictures representing travel destinations, furniture, health, love, and all of their deepest desires.

In addition to using pictures, they wrote down their dreams. Marilyn wanted to be further along in her speaking business and in writing her book. Eila dreamed of opening state-funded day care centers. Judie wanted to lose 50 pounds and buy beautiful clothes. Nancy wanted to write a book and get her Ph.D.

In addition to the Dream Big picture books and the written goals, they met monthly and spoke by phone weekly. In every meeting or conversation they worked on helping one another get through the discouragement and brainstorm ideas. Each member was reassured with words of confidence as if they had their dream already. "Eila, you are enjoying managing your day care centers with all the funding that you need. You are truly making a difference."

At the end of their meetings, they pray together. Also, every morning Marilyn spends ten minutes imagining her dreams and asking for help. She also said as her group progressed, they found themselves focusing less on material things and more on dreams that helped others. As soon as they switched to this "attitude of service" their dreams manifested more quickly.

Eila was the first to get results about five months after their initial meeting. The state of Ohio had approved funding for her day care centers and she was named Women Entrepreneur of the Year. Judie began losing weight. Nancy was in the middle of her book and back in school for her Ph.D. Marilyn is in the midst of her book now and busy with her seminar business.

Marilyn and her friends are average people just like you and me. With fears, hopes, and dreams. The only difference is they did not sit around and whine, "If only I could lose weight." "If only I could open some day care centers." They took ACTION. Just getting together and discussing our dreams ensures they are no longer inactive but actively working their way to us.

Speak Your Dreams—See Your Dreams

I remember when I began to Dream Big. One evening in about 1980, I was sitting in my cozy living room with some soft music playing in the background. As I sat there I wrote down all my longings and dreams and then recorded them on a cassette tape.

It felt wonderful as I said each of my dreams three times slowly, "I am now a nationally and internationally known speaker." "I now speak eight times a month." "I am now on my honeymoon in Greece." There were several more as well. At the end of the tape I added, "If these dreams are part of your divine plan for me, please guide me and show me the way." I listened to that tape often in my car. Three years later I began my speaking career. Every month for the first six months I spoke exactly eight times. No more—no less.

Did I stop there? No way. Now I was really committed. I began collecting pictures and words representing my dreams. Pictures of the Acropolis and the Greek Islands were included on my Dream Big board as I dreamed of my honeymoon. At the time, I wasn't dating a soul and there was no one in sight. That didn't stop me from dreaming big. I felt it was time to meet my divine life partner.

"Well, if I'm going to attract my life partner, I'd love to get married in the wine country." Pictures of grape vines and vineyards went on my Dream Big board along with the words Wine Country. For good measure, I cut out a picture of a woman's hand with a beautiful engagement ring. This was difficult because I was so afraid of disappointment. I asked, "Please bring me my life partner to help me learn how to grow and love."

I was living in a little studio apartment in San Francisco and money was tight. Clipping out pictures of beautiful homes was fun and adding them to my board was exciting and scary. But up they went—all kinds of houses and beautifully decorated sunny rooms. I thought, "One day I want to live in a house like that."

One day I saw pictures of books in the Book-of-the-Month Club. I remember asking myself, "I wonder if I can be an author?" Imagine me as an author. No way, I don't have the patience to sit down and write. But somewhere deep inside me, Sparkles said, "Yes, Barbara, you can do this—go ahead and dream." Once again, I realized I was getting direct spiritual guidance.

So I clipped pictures of books and glued them on the board with a picture of me holding a book. I added more pictures and when I finished I started crying. Have you ever wanted something so bad it hurts to think you might not get it? Well, I particularly wanted the love I deserved.

I remember looking at my board often and making it come alive. As I ate dinner by myself I stared at the pictures. I saw myself walking down the aisle of a beautiful lawn in St. Helena, California, on my wedding day. I felt the ocean breezes of Mykynos, Greece, on my honeymoon holding hands with my new husband. I imagined autographing my books and watching the sunset from the deck of my new house.

It was all so real and wonderful, but I still felt afraid. I asked for help, "Please help me not to doubt my dreams. Fill me with the faith and guidance I need to trust and listen to you." I kept hearing, "Have faith, Barbara. Don't give up." For five years nothing happened. I felt discouraged, but I never gave up hope and desire.

Six years after I completed my Dream Big board amazing things started to happen. Although I had a good job as a regional sales manager with a major company, the entrepreneurial spirit came over me. I decided to pursue my dream of becoming a professional speaker.

After the first year in business, I had enough money to put a down payment on a lovely home—all by myself. Three months after I moved in my new home, guess who I met? Bob, my loving, kind, supportive husband. He also loves the vineyards, so we got married at Meadowood Resort in St. Helena, California. Guess where we honeymooned? You got it—the Greek Islands. I even got to use my frequent flyer mileage for the plane tickets!

Two years after I met Bob a wonderful woman, Dominique, ran up to me after a speech on customer service. She said, "Great ideas—if you write them down, I'll publish it." I explained I had no manuscript or book proposal and had never written a book before. She replied, "No problem, I'm a publisher. I'll send you a contract and you have one year to write your book."

Five Star Service Solutions was published a year later. I'll never forget the day the first copy came in the mail. It was magical. Bob and I went out to dinner to celebrate and I was flying high.

Be Persistent and Don't Give Up

By now you may be saying, "Barbara, you're just lucky." I don't believe in luck, as I mentioned earlier in the book. I do believe strongly that, with persistence, courage, hard work and spiritual guidance, we can live the life we imagine and deserve. Dreaming big is not easy. I had many obstacles and disappointments along the way. What kept me going, however, was the clear picture of my future. Without my dreams and strong faith, I doubt I could have kept moving forward.

What about you? Whatever you're dreaming, it's not big enough. You need to reinforce your dreams with constant verbal, visual, and auditory reminders. And, if you're spiritually inclined, lots of prayer or affirmations.

> *Whatever you're dreaming,*
> *it's not big enough.*

Don't let doubt, fear and lack of faith stop you from dreaming big. You may imagine your dream and then your fearful voice asks, "How will you do that?" *How* is one of the most misunderstood words in the English language and can be a dream killer. When you begin to Dream Big, typically you don't have a clue "how" it will happen. Your job is to imagine it and trust the details will unfold later.

Ask "When" Instead of "How" or "If"

Let's imagine you are a close friend of mine. We're having dinner at a restaurant and you excitedly announce, "My dream is to leave my job and have a successful publicity company of my own." I look at you and in a challenging tone say, "How are you going to do that?" At this point you have a "big dream" but aren't clear on the details. My asking you "how" at this fragile stage, however, may discourage you from moving forward.

Again, focus on keeping your dream alive and trust that the *how* will come later. If we all had to know *how* everything will happen, none of us will ever dream again. A tip I have is to get into the habit of saying "when I" instead of "if I": "When I am promoted to district manager, I will hold a big sales rally." "When I take my family to our vacation in Disneyland, we'll have a ball." Remember, avoid words that fill you with doubt.

> *Get into the habit of saying,*
> *"when I" instead of "if I."*

Now it's your turn to Dream Big!

Summary of Key Points

■ Your dreams are *waiting* to happen.

■ Help others achieve their dreams.

■ Use pictures and an audiotape to keep your dreams alive.

■ Ask your spiritual source for guidance and direction.

■ Don't ask "how"—just dream.

■ Whatever you're dreaming, it's not big enough.

Exercise: Five-Minute Joy Booster

Every morning this week before you get out of bed, prop up the pillows, sit back, and take a few minutes to imagine one of your dreams. Then either say a little prayer, an affirmation, or read one of the quotes at the end of this section.

Exercise: My Ideal Life

In your Dream Big workbook, write at the top of a page My Ideal Life. Now start writing everything down in the present tense. This can be any length from one to six or seven pages or more. The key is not the length but the specific details and exciting language. This is your life, your story, so be colorful. For example, "I'm so happy in my lovely white Victorian home. Sitting on the big wide porch on summer evenings is such fun and so relaxing. I can smell the scent of the roses and heather. The sunlight streams through the big windows and I love cooking in my country kitchen. I'm surrounded by my family and friends and feel loved and supported."

"I'm now enjoying my ideal job as a successful meeting professional for a Fortune 1000 company. Retreats, sales conferences and award functions are all planned by me at exotic destinations. The people I work with are wonderful, I get to see new places, and I'm well paid and appreciated."

Keep writing until you run out of ideas. Feel free to go back and add to your Dream Big life story. As you write you may find Ms. Misery trying to discourage you with lots of negative comments. Just say, "Thank you for sharing," and keep dreaming big and writing.

Note: Don't forget to ask for help and guidance from your spiritual source. For example, write down: Dear _____, fill me with the faith and confidence to listen to your guidance and direction as I follow your divine plan for my happiness.

Exercise: Make a Dream Big Board or Book

Begin collecting pictures and words that excite you and represent all the dreams you wrote in your workbook for the previous ideal life exercise. Treat yourself to a stack of new magazines—perhaps travel, sports, decorating, investments, parenting, or bridal magazines will inspire you. Also, cut out words that are meaningful to you—love, health, friends, and so forth. Don't forget to add some acknowledgment of your spiritual faith as well. Go to an art supply store and get a big board for your pictures. Alternatively, you can use a three-ring binder and create a Dream Big book. Select a day when you are relaxed and begin cutting out the pictures and gluing them on your board or in your book. Feel free to add any later. Look at your dream board or book frequently.

Dream Big Group Members or Partner

Play the What's New game. Imagine it's five years in the future and you achieved many of the dreams on your board. Ask each group member or your dream partner "what's new" and share what you wrote down in your journal as if you have it now. For example, "I'm happily married to a wonderful woman, and my new job as a senior marketing director is fantastic."

Message for the Spiritually Inclined

If you ever doubt your dream is coming to you or you're feeling a bit discouraged, read the following words excerpted from the *Daily Word* for encouragement.

If a mountain stands in your way, climb it. If a river flows between you and where you need to be, build a bridge to get across. Nothing can stand in the way of your dreams with the power of God or _____ to back you up. With God's or _____ help, your dreams can become a reality!

■ ■ ■

You will say to this mountain, move from here to there, and it will move. (Matthew 17:20)

■ ■ ■

I ask with confidence and belief, knowing that God or _____will answer my prayers.

God or _____is my prosperity, blessing me richly in every way.

Step 6: Act As If—Take Your First Step

Now a warning. You may be feeling confident and excited. Hey, my dreams are in progress and all I have to do is wait patiently. Not exactly. There is a significant difference between those who Dream Big and those who truly *believe* in their dreams.

Demonstrate Commitment

If I said, "Demonstrate that you believe your dream will come true," what would you do to convince me? We've all heard the saying, "Fake it till you make it." The principle of *acting as if* is similar. In Step 5 you focused on specific dreams you'd like to create. In Step 6 you must now *act as if* you already have your dream to show your commitment.

Imagination is like a seed and it must be watered if it is to yield a harvest. What are you going to do while you're waiting for your dream to manifest? You are going to take action by letting your imagination kick into high gear. In week six, you'll begin taking some baby steps toward your dream and demonstrating your faith and commitment.

If you recall in Step 5, Tim wanted to help his sales rep achieve his dream of owning a condo. At the time it seemed impossible because of insufficient income. Most people would probably stop right there. No income—no condo. Why even bother dreaming when we don't have the money. Tim, however, remembered how important it is to *act as if* we expect our dream to happen.

Make Believe

Tim referred his rep to a real estate agent and suggested he start looking to get an idea of what he wanted and the purchase prices. Looking at condos and imagining owning one was a powerful demonstration of faith. Then together they figured out how much more he would have to earn to afford the condo. Between the pictures of the condo and the excitement of looking with a realtor, his rep actually felt his dream moving toward him. By *acting as if* and *making believe* he accelerated the process and was able to buy his condo.

Today managers need to remember to motivate people by focusing on their dreams.

Believe in Miracles

Let's do a little soul searching. Would you have the courage, faith, and desire to look at condos or houses if you didn't have the money? Does it seem silly or irrational? If so, I'm asking you to put logic and fears aside and truly expect the best. I'm also asking you to believe in miracles. Believe in your dreams like Dayle Dunn and Carl Mehler did.

When I met Dayle and Carl in 1987, Dayle was a training professional and Carl was an architect. They are a happily married couple who love life and art. They dreamed of owning an art gallery and living by the ocean. In 1993 they moved into their dream home on the ocean, where they also have a spectacular art gallery. How did they do it? I can assure you it was not luck. They did it by *acting as if* and moving toward their dream.

One day, Dayle and Carl playfully discussed, "Wouldn't it be fun to totally change our lives and live our dream? Imagine if we were gallery owners, surrounded by art and living by the ocean." The more they talked the more excited they got until they finally decided to pursue the gallery.

Within two weeks they took their first *act as if* step and contacted realtors in Half Moon Bay, California. All the realtors said it couldn't be done. To build an art gallery in a residence and get the sewer and other necessary permits was nearly impossible. Now many people might have stopped there and said, "Well, I guess it's not supposed to be." But not Dayle and Carl. They continued to look on their own and found the ideal property on the ocean zoned for both residential and commercial use.

Next they put their own lovely house on the market and rented a small, one-bedroom apartment in Half Moon Bay. This gave them the opportunity to adjust to their new environment and to begin designing plans for their new art gallery and home. Long before the gallery was even designed they both went to art fairs to meet artists and see what kind of art they would display for sale.

Meanwhile, many banks turned down their loan request, finding their unique project undesirable. Finally, they found the ideal lender. Just when things were looking good, the planning commission considered declining the entire project. This was especially frustrating since they had worked hard making all the required changes to the property.

Did they give up? No way. They visited their neighbors and other business owners on the street and got their support in writing. Armed with a model of the project, slides, and support letters, the planning commission unanimously approved their art gallery.

I remember attending the opening gala of the Dunn-Mehler Gallery with Bob and sharing in their joy. They were glowing with happiness as they proudly gave us a tour of the spectacular art gallery connected to their dream house.

Carl said the reason they had no fear was they were not attached to the outcome. They had lived in a small apartment for a year and a half and had a great time. "If things didn't work out, we'd sell the property and move back to an apartment," Carl explained. "Things are not important to us. The fun is in trying and doing. Dayle and I are energized by the people we meet and the ocean, working with art, and enjoying ourselves. If we don't succeed it's not a failure—it's an adventure."

Here's an interesting note: Ten years before they bought the property at the beach, Carl was impressed with an art gallery in Chicago. He obtained a poster-size picture of the inside of the gallery and kept that picture above his desk for years. Now he and Dayle are in their own special picture. The key is they consistently *acted as if* they expected their dream to work out. If you happen to be in Half Moon Bay, California, be sure to stop by the Dunn-Mehler Gallery and say hello.

For you skeptics, let me give you a personal example. Remember in Step 5, *Dream Big,* I mentioned I wanted to attract my divine mate. Recording my dream on audiotape and gluing pictures on my Dream Big board certainly helped keep my dream alive. But I still had to show faith and *act as if* I expected my dream to happen.

When I moved into my lovely new home as a single, I had a large walk-in closet with two built-in dressers and lots of poles for clothes. I put all my clothes in one dresser on the left and filled up half the pole space. The right hand dresser and pole space remained completely empty even though I could have easily used all the closet space. Why did I only use half the closet? Because I truly believed my divine mate was on the way, and I had to make space for this person in my life. My realtor thought I was crazy. Now I have the last laugh with an incredibly loving, devoted husband.

In addition, I kept one extra room, the den, completely empty because I imagined my partner as an entrepreneur like me in need of a home office. That empty room became Bob's office where he ran our consulting company activities before we moved to our new offices. By praying for my divine mate regularly and *acting as if* he were coming, I was rewarded with my wonderful husband.

Are You Willing to Work Hard?

Don't think it's easy; we must be willing to take a hard look at ourselves. Besides making my audiotape, using pictures, and leaving my closet half empty, I felt I had to get myself ready for my ideal mate. I sought out intensive personal counseling to identify any blocks or behaviors that were preventing me from having the close, intimate relationship I desired. It was a painful and vulnerable process—and the best thing I could have done.

I also sought out feedback from male friends and associates about how they perceived me. Guess what?

They were all surprised I was even interested in a relationship. One friend, Kurt, said, "You seem so happy and independent, as if you don't want or need a partner." What an eye-opener. Obviously, I had work to do. The hardest part for me was to admit I had no control and ask for help. I'm convinced the combination of my counseling, prayers, feedback, and *acting as if* all led to my soul mate, Bob.

Probably the biggest and most difficult *act as if* experience was when Bob and I bought our new dream house together. We both decided that one day, if we could afford it, we'd like to live in a really nice, large Mediterranean home with land, views, clay tile roof, and lots of light. In fact, we had pictures of our dream home on our board.

At the time we wanted to relocate to San Diego. We couldn't afford our dream home but were content to buy a nice tract home. While we were out looking, our realtor told us there were some really incredible houses on the market at distressed prices. He then proceeded to drive us to an area full of gorgeous, custom—Mediterranean—homes at practically half price.

When he pulled up in front of a beautiful home with columns, I felt a bit uncomfortable and whispered to Bob, "This is out of our league." As soon as we walked inside and I saw the canyon views, the arches, the tile floors, and the sunlight streaming in, I thought, "We belong here." The house was nearly twice the size of the tract houses we were considering.

Our realtor, Rick, said, "Let me see what I can do—make an offer." Bob and I offered what we wanted to pay on a much smaller tract house and considerably less than the asking price. I thought Rick would refuse to present our offer but he went for it. We prayed for guidance: "If this house is meant for us and we can easily afford it, please let the builder accept our bid. If it is not in your divine plan now, please let the deal fall through and we will happily move into the tract house."

The brand new house had been on the market for three years. The builder was in financial trouble and needed to pay off his construction loan. He accepted our low offer, which allowed us to move into our dream home about ten years ahead of schedule. If we hadn't *acted as if* and actually walked inside some luxury homes, I doubt we'd be living in our dream house today.

Acting As If Is Fun

At first *acting as if* seems silly and even scary. With practice, it gets easier and playful, and becomes a way of life. All it is, is making believe and acting out your dreams. Don't delay—move toward your dreams and take a baby step.

The *act as if* principle is also powerful for creating prosperity—a feeling of plenty or abundance—in our lives. We have plenty of friends, plenty of love, and perhaps plenty of money. I'm convinced, however, that money by itself does not bring happiness. It is through our beliefs and reliance on our spiritual source that we can attain peace and prosperity. We are rewarded with a life filled with friends, love, health, vitality, spirituality, and most of all, a sense of well-being. We can *feel* prosperous without actually being prosperous.

Show Faith in Difficult Times

People don't seem to understand that to attract more prosperity they have to *act as if* they are prosperous. For instance, I met a young single mom who was working as a bank teller. Her husband left her, she had no family in the area, and money was very tight. Despite these difficult challenges, she purchased fresh flowers every week, which for her was an extravagance. "The flowers are a reminder that my life is blooming and I am only experiencing a temporary setback," she told me one day. What a great outlook on life's challenges. It is important to show our faith when money is tight and not focus on *scarcity*.

Do the Little Things

By this I mean leave a standard or generous tip in restaurants. Give generously at your church service or to those in need. Buy gourmet coffee now and then if it makes you feel good. By not obsessing over our tight financial situation and *acting as if* all is well, we are demonstrating our faith that all is well. I am *not* suggesting we buy or charge things we can't afford. Just do little things to keep our outlook hopeful and positive.

Acting as if means we need to adopt a "do it" mentality and avoid the "prove it" mentality. The "prove it" mentality means, "You show me first exactly how I can have my dream without any risk of failure." If Walt Disney had the "prove it" mentality, we'd never have Disneyland.

Are you ready to do it? Of course you are or you wouldn't be reading this book. What can you do to *act as if* your dream is coming? If you are interested in doing TV commercials, sign up for an acting class. If you are hoping for a big promotion, buy yourself a new briefcase. If you are dreaming of buying a special car, take one out for a test drive. If you want to go on a cruise, buy yourself a cruise outfit and save it for the trip. You get the idea! In other words, do something to show your commitment and faith. Beware of your fearful voice who will try to stop you and ask "how?" Remember, don't worry about the details. Just ask for guidance and help.

Following is a list of suggestions to help you feel prosperous and avoid scarcity thinking:

■ Give to your church or spiritual source.

■ Treat yourself to a massage.

■ Get a house cleaner periodically.

■ Get help with mowing the lawn or gardening.

■ Order a special glass of wine instead of the house brand.

■ Give money to a friend or family member in need without expecting payment.

■ Donate your time to help a friend or comfort someone.

■ Buy a little gift for a friend or loved one for no specific occasion.

■ Get "full serve" gasoline once in a while.

Avoid these *scarcity* activities:

■ Spending excessive energy on coupon clipping.

■ Driving out of your way to save a minimal amount of money on groceries.

■ Ordering the cheapest item on a menu.

■ Asking people to split an entree when you really want your own. (A friend of mine dated a guy who insisted they split an entree! Is that cheap or what?)

■ Undertipping for services.

■ Wearing old clothes or shoes you no longer enjoy.

Summary of Key Points

■ Imagination is like a seed and must be watered.

■ Demonstrate you believe your dream is in progress and *act as if*.

■ Adopt a *do it* mentality and avoid the *prove it* mentality.

■ Act prosperous and treat yourself and others well when money is tight.

Exercise: Five-Minute Joy Booster

Every morning this week before you get out of bed, prop up the pillows, sit back, and take a few minutes to imagine one of your dreams. Then either say a little prayer, an affirmation, or read one of the quotes at the end of this section.

Exercise: Act As If You Believe

In your Dream Big workbook, write at the top of a new page Act As If and the date. To get warmed up focus on one or two dreams and jot them down on the left, leaving extra space to write on the right side. Next, ask yourself, "If I know this dream is definitely on the way, what can I do to prepare and demonstrate my belief?" For example, long before I ever became a professional speaker I dreamed about it. I made it a goal and wanted to keep my dream alive and not get discouraged. One day, Sparkles said, "Go buy new luggage." Ms. Misery, my fearful voice, strongly objected with, "That's ridiculous, the luggage you have is just fine. Besides, you can't afford it." Sparkles said, "If you buy the luggage you'll get to use it as a speaker." I listened to Sparkles and remember the joy I felt when I took that luggage on my first speaking tour. Buying the luggage was my way of *acting as if* I already had my dream.

What can you do to take one or two action steps toward your dream? To *act as if* you already have it? Write it down now in your Dream Big journal and then DO IT!

Dream Big Group Members or Partner

Share one or two of your dreams and ideas of how you can *act as if*. Make a commitment to do something in the next month to move toward your dream. Get support and ideas from the group members or your dream partner.

Message for the Spiritually Inclined

The following affirmations are recommended for creating prosperity:

Dear Lord or _____, Show me the way to attract great abundance and be of service.

■ ■ ■

Dear Lord or _____, Let all that is mine by divine right come to me now as I fulfill my life plan according to Your wishes.

■ ■ ■

God or _____opens doors of opportunity to me and my faith leads me through them.

■ ■ ■

Whatever you ask for in prayer, believe that you have received it, and it will be yours. (Mark 11:24)

Imagine the Best—
Let's Practice the Process

Congratulations! In the last six weeks you have become one of a select group of people in the world to choose your future. You now have a powerful, proven six-step process to use any time you wish to bring your dreams into reality. In this section we'll review all of them to ingrain them in your mind.

Let's review:

Step 1: Welcome Wake-Up Calls—Pay Attention to the Guiding Signs

Step 2: Listen to Your Heart—Say "No" to Ms. Misery

Step 3: Test the Waters—Take the Risk Out of Risk

Step 4: Effort Less—Enjoy the Ride

Step 5: Dream Big—Imagine the Best That Can Happen

Step 6: Act As If—Take Your First Step

I'm sure by now your mind is full of exciting possibilities you'd like to create in your life. Let's choose your first dream and apply the six-step process straight through. This serves as a brief summary and gets you in the habit of using your new skills.

Right now imagine I snapped my fingers and instantly transformed you to your dream. What are you doing? Where are you? Whom are you with? Imagine every incredible detail. Please place the book down and see one of your dreams in vivid color. Now write it down in your Dream Big workbook and let's work our way through the steps.

Step 1: Welcome Wake-Up Calls— Pay Attention to the Guiding Signs

What obstacles come up in your mind when you imagine your dream? Have you been ignoring any wake-up calls or signs? Perhaps you are over-scheduled and feel you have no time to enjoy life. Or you may keep repeating the same obstacles or disappointments. Jot down all the guiding signs and look through your list. What can you do to move in a new direction?

Step 2: Listen to Your Heart—Say No to Ms. Misery

Imagine again you have your dream. Let your heart encourage you. Earlier, you gave a special name to your intuition. Please ask for support now: "Dear _____, Please encourage and assure me I deserve this dream. Guide me and show me the way. Remind me that with your help anything is possible." Note for the spiritually inclined: This is a very powerful prayer when you direct your request to the Lord or a higher power. Be patient for the answers to your request. Try to quiet Ms. Misery or your fearful voice.

Step 3: Test the Waters—Take the Risk Out of Risk

Now that you've gotten some inspiration and direction from your spirit, fear is likely to crop up. It's important to minimize the risk by understanding fear. Fear in my opinion is simply "imagination and worry out of control." Therefore, to take the risk out of risk ask yourself, "What's the worst that can happen?" Write down all your fears and list all of your options. List some possible action steps and support mechanisms you can put in place to avoid getting discouraged.

Step 4: Effort Less—Enjoy the Ride

At this point it's natural for some frustration and anxiety to arise. Now that we are moving toward our dream we must "let it happen." If we are too attached to the outcome we may sabotage our progress. Take a hard look at all the people and situations in your life that are not supporting your dream. Perhaps you are trying to control the process instead of enjoying it. Dreaming big is meant to be fun. If you are efforting and struggling it's time to trust, relax, and let go.

Step 5: Dream Big—Imagine the Best
That Can Happen

The previous four steps encourage you to listen, believe, and move toward your dreams. So now ask yourself the big question: "What's the best that can happen?" It's important to fuel the fire of your dream. Write it down, make an audiotape, and begin collecting pictures for your Dream Big board. Act quickly to keep the momentum going.

Step 6: Act As If—Take Your First Step

To truly set your dream in motion you must take a step and *act as if* your dream is imminent. What step will you take based on the dream you chose? If you want to write a book, sign up for a class. If you are dreaming of a new car, take it for a test drive. And remember don't worry about "how" it will happen. Just make believe and have a wonderful time. Feel the emotion and exhilaration as you anticipate having your dream.

Pitfalls to Avoid

■ Expecting immediate results—be patient.

■ Trying to logically figure out "how" things will happen.

■ Letting your "fear" voice discourage you. Fight back!

■ Listening to negative people.

■ Skipping the Dream Big board exercise.

■ Taking no action step—remember to *act as if*.

■ Not asking for spiritual guidance.

Keep Your Dream Alive

The most difficult thing for many people is keeping their dream alive. After all, it may take one, five, or ten years. The four most powerful things you can do are:

1. Look at your Dream Big board daily but at least once a week.
2. Practice Step 6, *acting as if*, and do something to reinforce your dream.
3. Organize a Dream Big support group or get a Dream Big partner.
4. Practice the *daily joy booster*.

Summary of Key Points

■ Practice the six-step *make it happen* process.

■ Avoid pitfalls.

■ Keep your dream alive.

Exercise: Five-Minute Joy Booster

Every morning this week before you get out of bed, prop up the pillows, sit back, and take a few minutes to imagine one of your dreams. Then either say a little prayer, an affirmation, or read one of the quotes at the end of this section.

Dream Big Group Members or Partner

Share one dream each and verbally walk through the six-step process to reinforce them. Ask group members for help.

PART III

Share Your Dream— Savor the Journey

Create Cappuccino Moments
—Enjoy Your Journey

*The greatest regret of the terminally ill is, "I
made a living, but I never really lived."*
—Dr. Elizabeth Kubler-Ross

Are you making a living or living your life? To "live"
your life implies action, movement, excitement.

The six-step *make it happen* process you've discovered in this book is designed to make your life more
rewarding, fun, and alive. And when I say your *life* I don't
just mean your *work*. You are meant to enjoy all that life
has to offer.

Are You Enjoying the Feast?

Picture your life as an incredible feast. Spread before you is a banquet table with every possible delicacy
and food you can imagine. Sumptuous seafood, warm
breads, luscious desserts, assorted cheeses, unusual ap-
petizers, and much more. What will you choose? Despite
the wide variety and choices available, you may look for
your usual broiled chicken. That's it. You just want broiled
chicken.

The broiled chicken may represent your work or career. Sometimes our choice is routine and done out of habit.
The challenge is to make educated and informed choices
based on our values and priorities. You are meant to live a

life that is meaningful, fulfilling, and exciting. "Live" is an action word. Are you *living* your life or *doing* your life?

Your life's menu is full of choices to enjoy—spirituality, love, family, financial security, relaxation, social activities, and many more. If you only taste broiled chicken and never indulge in the other courses on the menu, you may be missing out. Your life may be one dimensional, lacking in richness and depth.

Lighten Up

Most of us take life much too seriously. In our desire to achieve our future goals, we miss out on the joys of today. Often our lives are reduced to one big "to do" list. Meanwhile, the days, months, and years race by.

Earlier you took the Life Satisfaction Index. How did you score on number 4, "relaxation and social"? Again, you must take the time to "live" your life, not to "do" your life. Achieving balance is an important part of happiness. You must find a way to blend your leisure time, family and work responsibilities, spiritual development, and social activities. Most people blame their inability to relax on a huge list of responsibilities and a shortage of time.

Outsource to Create Time

It's common practice for businesses to outsource certain responsibilities such as bookkeeping, publicity, and marketing. There is no reason why we can't find a way to seek assistance by outsourcing as well. Think of all the chores and responsibilities we all have to take care of, from grocery shopping to calling repair people, from housecleaning to paying bills. These are major time and energy drainers. Imagine what might happen if we opened our mind to other possibilities.

For example, for ten years, Bob and I have always had help doing our errands. Twice a month Marge comes over and goes to the grocery store, the dry cleaner, the shoemaker, the hardware store, and so forth. When she gets back, she puts everything away. This incredible time-saver only costs us seven dollars an hour. For four hours, it costs us twenty-eight dollars to get help and gives us time to enjoy life more. Rather than being stuck in traffic and waiting in lines doing errands, we can truly enjoy our precious weekends.

In addition, often your errand person will have time to make some phone calls, locate a repairman, track down that special cable you need. Marge started out doing errands and now pays our bills twice a month. Last year she found a shop to fix our Dust Buster and took care of it. As a result, our life is much less stressful. Plus, Marge is a delight who loves to provide a valuable service. I love having a "wife" to help me!

After a keynote speech, Diane, a dental assistant, approached me and said, "I'm learning to relax and get help. I hate to iron so I found this college student who does all my ironing twice a month for six dollars an hour. My husband and I skip a dinner out and budget for it." Another gentlemen who is quite handy, told me he'd rather pay for a handyman to free up his time. He wants to spend extra time with his kids. My husband, Bob, occasionally has a college student, Jeremy, help with cleaning the patio and garage. As a result, he's less stressed and doesn't have to feel guilty about household chores.

My friend, Agatha, is a busy sales professional and Charlie, her husband, works hard as a pharmacist. As two professionals getting chores done is a real challenge. To free up time, they have all their laundry done by a professional service that picks up and delivers. Agatha said, "I don't want to spend the extra twenty minutes to drop it off and twenty minutes to pick it up. It's been great and I'd rather give up eating out, buying clothes, or do without something to budget for it."

Believe You Deserve It

Beware of falling into the trap of, "I have so much to do I couldn't possibly go on a picnic this Saturday." Or, "No one can clean my house as well as I can. Besides, they might rip me off." Help is available for all of us if we believe we deserve it. I can hear some of you saying, "It's easy for you, Barbara, because you can afford it." Over and over again I'm struck by how many people get in the trap of "thinking lack."

Even if you are on a tight budget, start keeping track of how money slips through your fingers. Tom, a branch manager in a bank, told me he figured out that in a month if he and his wife skipped one Saturday night out to the movies and a casual dinner, skipped a few cappuccinos and the impulse CD purchase, they could get a house cleaner twice a month.

If you are willing to give up something "optional" in your life, there's a good chance you can budget for the help you deserve. No one said you have to be superman or superwoman and do it all yourself. I don't know about you, but I value my time very much and I would rather give up a meal or purchasing physical possessions if it means more life enjoyment. Give some serious thought to "outsourcing" and life may become a bit more enjoyable.

Whether it's a house cleaner, errand assistant, gardener, or bill-paying service, try an ad in your local newspaper. Bob and I have found all our help that way.

Also, nearly all of the colleges have job posting boards. Most of the people who are available tend to be students, moms, or semi-retired people who just want to earn a little extra.

What I'm really saying is consider "outsourcing" any chores that drain your time. Help is available if we can get over the I-have-to-do-it-all superwoman or superman syndrome.

Allow for Cappuccino Moments

Now, let's suppose you get assistance and successfully create more free time. The question is, "Can you really be present and enjoy your free time?" Have you ever worked frantically and then tried to squeeze in a vacation? Then on vacation you're on the beach thinking of all the things you have to do back home. You're unable to be present to the moment. It's important to take some *cappuccino moments* to nurture yourself when you're not able to take a vacation. A cappuccino moment can be a hike, picnic, hot bath, massage, short walk, good book— anything that will allow you to stop and appreciate the present moment. Notice what is around you, stop your mind, and open your heart.

With all the demands on your time, I know it's difficult to carve out time just to play. Make it a priority and plan it. You must rejuvenate and re-energize your juices. Recently Bob and I started looking at our calendars and blocking out specific Saturdays or Sundays in advance for "play" days. On a "play" day we do not do one bit of work or errands, just recreation from morning to night. It was hard at first, but now we look forward to it and find we are far more refreshed and productive the day after.

How often do we get in the routine of doing the same old things? Picnic in the same park, breakfast at the same restaurant. Instead, start viewing your free time as "precious" and not to be wasted. It's important to "plan ahead" and be creative.

One Sunday afternoon Bob said, "Let's just get in the car and drive to the new Four Seasons Resort Aviara in Carlsbad for a snack." Not being the spontaneous type, I was a bit resistant and then I thought, "What a great idea." We had a lovely thirty-minute drive there.

The hotel is spectacular with beautiful landscaping, panoramic views, and palm trees everywhere. The patio poolside cafe with its iron furniture, colorful umbrellas, and great view had a charming ambiance. The menu was reasonable and the food delicious. So for the same price as eating at our regular local cafe, Bob and I spent a couple of hours crashing a five-star resort. Another delightful *cappuccino moment*.

A successful and fun-loving friend of mine, Jim Cathcart, treats himself to breakfast out alone each week day at his favorite cafe. Jim said, "It gives me time to think, reflect, and focus before I go into the office." Jim is the one who gave me the phrase *cappuccino moment* and he certainly views his private breakfast time as just that.

Beware of "predictability" and "routine" in your personal life. Make an effort to see new things and create new experiences. It's important to feel good about yourself and enjoy all the gifts life has to offer.

Let Nature Nurture Your Soul

Nature and spirituality are probably the two best ways to make sure you are enjoying the journey of life. It's important to experience your life and nurture your soul.

For me, watching and listening to the sound of crashing waves totally relaxes every muscle in my body and stills my mind. Listening to birds chirping and watching them soar in the sky can lift my spirits. Reading some spiritual quotes or bible passages also helps me feel peaceful and focus on the present. What about you? It's important to identify what will fill your soul with joy and satisfaction.

The point is while you're waiting for your big dreams to manifest, remember to create *cappuccino moments*, preferably daily or at least weekly. Although this book is titled *Dream Big!*, we must never forget all the *little* wonders and dreams we can experience.

A touching moment with a child or an elderly relative. Curling up with a good book. Allowing yourself to enjoy a wonderful massage or lunch with a friend. All your little dreams and self-nurturing will prepare you to receive your big dream.

My five-minute joy booster you've been doing the last six weeks is a great way to start each day. Keep something uplifting or spiritual to read by your bedside. In the morning, do not get out of bed until you sit back, fluff your pillows, and fill yourself with words of beauty or encouragement. Ponder the words. Imagine your dreams. Say a short prayer asking for your day to be full of wonder, joy, and guidance.

On a special vacation in Italy, I remember reading a spiritual note each morning while looking out at the countryside in Tuscany. At the time, I also had some business issues causing me concern. After enjoying my joy booster each morning, however, I felt an immediate sense of well-being.

Be Childlike and Lighten Up

Children can also teach us a powerful lesson. Each day they look with wonder and curiosity at some new discovery. Unconcerned about time, they lose themselves for hours at play. Uninhibited, they question and challenge authority, always asking, "Why?" They risk by being playful, open and silly. Remember when you were a child at play—painting, coloring or building blocks with no sense of worry or time pressures. You can create that now. Last year I bought a child's watercolor paint set with primary colors and a big pad of artists paper. Hours went by as I painted colorful drawings that looked like they were painted by a five year old. I had a ball and felt so free—so childlike.

Are you silly at times? I hope so. When your favorite song comes on the radio in your car, are you able to sing along with gusto? One day driving along the Interstate 5 in San Diego, I was worrying about a business appointment. All of a sudden one of my favorite songs came on the radio—*Respect* by Aretha Franklin. I got so excited, I started singing aloud and bobbing my head. A car pulled up on my left and the woman on the passenger side just stared at me in disbelief with her mouth gaping open. I thought, "Party pooper," and just kept singing happily along, as if I was performing live with great animation.

Then a sleek BMW pulled up on my right and I realized the driver was singing along to the same song and enjoying it as much as I was. He gave me a quick thumbs up, nodded his head in approval, and drove off. I just started laughing out loud. It made my day. "Now what was I worrying about a minute ago?" I wondered. My meeting was a little pimple on the journey of life. One song put it all in perspective. Now my motto is, be silly and *lighten up.*

Let's rediscover how to put the gifts of play, wonder, and curiosity back in your life.

Summary of Key Points

■ View your life as an incredible feast and sample all the courses.

■ Take the time to "live" your life, not "do" your life.

■ Seek the assistance you deserve.

■ Take *cappuccino moments.*

■ Embrace nature and spirituality.

■ Be silly and lighten up.

Exercise: Five-Minute Joy Booster

Every morning this week before you get out of bed, prop up the pillows, sit back, and take a few minutes to imagine one of your dreams. Then either say a little prayer, an affirmation, or read one of the quotes at the end of this section.

Exercise: My *Cappuccino Moments*

In your Dream Big workbook, label a new page, My Cappuccino Moments, and date it. Now think of some things you love to do that you haven't done in awhile. Just keep writing and writing. Look at your list and pick one item and commit to do it within the week or month. Determining a "time frame" is very important. Cross it off and pick another one and continue until you get in the habit of taking *cappuccino moments* to enjoy your wonderful life. Ask your family and friends to help you.

Exercise: I Deserve Assistance

In your Dream Big workbook, label a new page, *I Deserve Help,* and date it. On the left side, list all of the responsibilities, chores and activities in your life that you would love to eliminate or get someone else to do. For example, I dislike housecleaning, gardening, shopping, ironing, washing my car, mowing the lawn, and so forth. On the right, next to each item, jot down an idea of how you can get assistance. See the following example.

I dislike the following:	How I can get assistance:
Housecleaning	Get a house cleaner
Mowing the lawn	Ask the neighbor's teenage son
Paying bills	Get a college student to help
Cleaning the barbecue or patio furniture	Ask my teenage children

Dream Big Group Members or Partner

Share what you dislike doing and make a commitment with a date of when you will get the help you deserve.

Message for the Spiritually Inclined

If you are having difficulty taking time for yourself, let the following words inspire you:

I will try to remember that when I take time for myself, I have much more to offer myself, my work, and those around me.

—Anne Wilson Schaef

■ ■ ■

Normal day, let me be aware of the treasure you are. Let me learn from you, love you, bless you before you depart. Let me not pass you by in quest of some rare and perfect tomorrow. Let me hold you while I may, for it may not always be so. One day I shall dig my nails into the earth, or bury my face in the pillow, or stretch myself taut, or raise my hands to the sky and want, more than all the world, your return.

—Mary Jean Iron

■ ■ ■

Laughter is an expression of my joyous soul.

—Excerpted from the *Daily Word*

■ ■ ■

Dear Lord or _____, Thank You for helping me create more joyful times and balance in my life.

Be Grateful—Experience the Joy of Giving

Over the years I've noticed a very interesting phenomenon. Two people can be very committed about applying the six-step Dream Big process and get very different results. Often the individual who is creating dreams easily is focused on helping others. The individual interested only in their own dreams tends to get minimal results.

Be "We" Focused

If we want to succeed in our own life, we need to help others succeed. Beware of being "me" focused instead of "we" focused. People who are "me" focused tend to be "takers" and people who are "we" focused tend to be "givers." The givers in life enjoy making people happy. Serving others comes naturally to them. As a result, these people are blessed with good fortune.

Be Thankful for What You Do Have

Regardless of whether you create all of your dreams—just a few or none—be grateful for the life you do live. It's so easy to whine about what you don't have. Remember to express your gratitude for all of your gifts by sharing your good fortune and time with others.

Years ago a friend of mine, Marianna Nunes, suggested that I contribute to the source of my spiritual strength by giving generously. As Bob and I began to realize how blessed we are, we were filled with a sense of gratitude. Now, regardless of our financial situation, we give to our church or other needy charities. It's our way of saying, "Thank you, God, for all the incredible guidance and direction You provide." As a result, we continue to prosper and grow. Marianna passed away while I was writing this book and I will always be thankful for her wise guidance and friendship.

Is giving and sharing a part of your life?

The Gift of Appreciation

When you help an elderly person with the groceries, volunteer at your kid's school, or take the time to listen to a distraught friend, you demonstrate the spirit of service. Let's ask, "How can I make someone smile today?" (Look at the list Seven Easy Ways to Demonstrate Appreciation and the Spirit of Service at the end of this section.)

Appreciation is a gift. And no one gives the gift better than my friend and colleague, Mary Marcdante, who speaks about communication, stress management, and the power of appreciation. Mary is always looking for ways to praise or compliment the people around her.

Many years ago, Mary was conducting an image workshop at the private home of a teacher in Milwaukee. The teacher had invited five of her coworkers to attend so Mary could provide suggestions on how they could improve their presence and appearance. It was a warm enough day for Mary to work outside, and as she walked into the blooming backyard, she greeted the backs of two of the women admiring the gardens. When they heard Mary say hello, they turned around to respond in kind. What happened next is permanently etched in Mary's mind.

The first woman walked toward her and said, "Hello." Mary shook her hand. The second woman turned around to face her directly but remained at a distance. Mary noticed this woman's face was horribly scarred and she was missing part of her right cheekbone and the protective socket underneath her left eye.

Mary was shocked as she searched for what to say next. She told me she often says silently when confronted with these kinds of situations, "Mom, what do I say?" (Mary claims her mother was the queen of appreciation.) The next words out of her mouth were, "You have the most beautiful smile. What's your name?" The woman's body relaxed as she walked to accept Mary's extended hand for a handshake. It was apparent that, given her appearance, "Jane" was relieved to receive a genuine—and likely very rare—compliment so quickly, rather than a look of terror or disgust.

As the day was coming to a close, Mary explained how to accept a compliment with a simple, "Thank you," since most people resist with words of deflection. She then finished her work by offering a positive comment about each person's style. When she came to the woman with the scarred face, Mary said, "You have the most captivating smile and calm and loving presence," to which "Jane" responded, "Thank you." As Mary was saying good bye, Jane stopped her in front of everyone, and asked, "Before you leave, could you just say those compliments one more time to each of us so we can hear them again?"

Mary finished telling me about her experience and said, "So many people are literally starved for appreciation and recognition of what they value in themselves. One of the most magnificent gifts we give another is the acknowledgment of their own greatness that they are unable to speak about themselves. Moments of appreciation are always in front of you if you're willing to look for them. And once you are the recipient of, 'one good turn does bring another and makes both of you feel good,' you go looking for ways to appreciate others."

During college Mary worked at the post office, and learned that the standard procedure for oversized mail is to leave a yellow reminder in the recipient's mailbox saying that the oversized mail could be retrieved at the local postal station. This is often a challenge as one has to work around postal hours, lack of parking spaces, and long lines, as is the case where Mary now lives in southern California.

One afternoon a couple years ago, Mary was picking up her mail and noticed the postman delivering the mail to all the condominium boxes. Mary started up a conversation and said, "Hi. I'm Mary Marcdante. I used to work for the post office and want you to know how much I appreciate the hard work that you do. Please tell me your name." The postal carrier looked surprised and said, "Thank you. My name's Gary. I'm not used to people telling me they appreciate what I do." Mary's praise was music to his ears.

The following week, Mary noticed that when packages arrived that were too big to fit in the small postal box, they were returned to the postal station, as usual. However, her larger packages were delivered to her doorstep, along with the rest of her mail, which has continued to this day.

Recently Mary was preparing to go out of town and was anxiously awaiting the arrival— by mail—of a package of medication that she needed to take with her on her trip. The package didn't arrive the day before her departure. The day she was leaving, Mary knew the mailman wouldn't arrive until three o'clock, two hours past the time she would depart for the airport. However, she also knew that Gary might be in the area delivering mail in the morning, so she went hunting for mail trucks.

About a half mile away, Mary sighted a postal truck, only to find it empty. She left a note: "Gary, if there's any chance you might be able to locate a package of medication for me and could get it to me by one o'clock this afternoon, before I leave for the airport, I'd be so grateful! Please call me and she left her number. Thanks, Mary."

At twelve-thirty Mary's phone rang. It was Gary. He said the package was nowhere to be found, and he even apologized for not being able to find it. He also said that if he came across it, he'd do what he could to get it to her before she left.

Mary was shocked he even returned the call, given that he hadn't found the package. She said, "You're amazing! Thank you so much for taking the time to call. At least next time I'll know where to find your truck!"

He said, "Oh, that's not my truck. Another driver found your note and called me with your message." Unbelievable!

Look at the amazing level of service her postal carrier was excited enough to provide as a result of her appreciation. We all have this powerful gift to give others, and it costs nothing but time and the desire to see others smile.

When I asked Mary why so many people don't praise others more often she gave five common reasons.

1. They forget.
2. They think people will get a big head.
3. It makes the giver or receiver uncomfortable.
4. It doesn't change anything.
5. Society doesn't reward praise with money.

"And yet, the oddest part about all of this," Mary said, "is that when I ask people what they most want from the people they love and the people they work with, the most common response is 'to be appreciated.' Verbal appreciation costs no money and is one of the longest lasting gifts we give another...and more importantly, everyone wants and needs it."

What about you? Are you hoarding your gift of appreciation? I believe strongly that every one of us should be committed to make one person smile everyday. It can be a family member, a coworker, a waitress, or a total stranger. Look around you and know that you can make a difference.

Encourage, Mentor, and Reward at Work

The spirit of giving is also needed in the workplace. Imagine the workplace of the future as more sensitive, nurturing, and caring. Most of us want work that is fulfilling and satisfying. We want to make a contribution at work and be acknowledged and respected. Unfortunately, some CEOs and managers don't understand the power of putting their people first. An obsession with profits and customers causes them to overlook their greatest assets— their people.

Whether you are an employee, manager, business owner, or company president, you can make a profound difference by encouraging and mentoring others. Instead of focusing on only the company vision or your own agenda, you can help your associates grow and achieve their personal vision.

Be a Servant Leader

Mike Maslak is a friend who also happens to be the president of North Island Federal Credit Union in San Diego. When he first joined the credit union, staff morale was low. Mike had his hands full as he was brought on to turn North Island into a high-performing, member-focused credit union.

Mike shared this with me: "I felt the most important thing to do initially was to listen to the staff and start addressing their needs. I had to earn their trust and respect while I implemented new employee- and member-focused programs, which became the basis for the new corporate culture."

Within a short period of time he was visiting with small groups of employees in Fireside Chats. He invited staff to serve on action teams and acted on their recommendations. Climate surveys were conducted to monitor the staff perception of the new culture.

Mike is big on communication, recognition, and reward. I spoke at his Annual Vision Meeting and watched in awe as four hundred employees enthusiastically participated. All staff members received profit-sharing checks handed to them that evening. Some special employees and managers were personally recognized and rewarded for their exceptional performance. It's clear that the staff at North Island feel important and appreciated. As a result, the credit union is thriving.

Mike's leadership philosophy is really quite simple: "Put your people first and success will follow." He truly enjoys sharing his success with his teammates. Mike practices "servant leadership," considering it a privilege and honor to lead and serve his staff.

"In short, being a benefactor is an extraordinary 'natural high'—as exhilarating as the legendary 'runners high,'" Mike commented. "The bonus is when the individual involved doesn't even expect it! Now that's an ethereal experience worth having and cherishing forever."

Be Interested in Your Staff

Many years ago I had a wonderful administrative assistant, Linda. Although her work was excellent, I sensed that she was not totally fulfilled working for me. There was a subtle edge of sadness and frustration about her. One day in a relaxed, spontaneous conversation, she said, "You know it's not easy working for you, Barbara."

Well at that point I thought, "Oh no, she probably thinks I'm a demanding boss or a tyrant."

Linda then explained, "It's obvious you love what you do, you love your life, and you found your purpose. Plus, in your work you encourage other people to pursue their dreams. Therefore, I'm constantly reminded that I am not fulfilling my life plan or doing anything about my photography." At the time Linda was passionate about her hobby of nature photography. Her work was excellent. I even had one of her photos hanging in our office.

I asked her, "What would be a sign of success for you with your photography? And dream really big—don't hold back."

She excitedly said, "A private gallery showing of my work where I can invite all my friends." What a great dream, I thought. I was proud of her; I could tell this was a stretch.

I encouraged her to take her work around to galleries that coming Friday, her day off. She was understandably skeptical. I reminded her she had to *act as if* she was a successful photographer to move toward her dream. After all, there really was no risk. The worst that could happen is she'd be politely declined by the gallery owners. Linda had about five or six galleries in mind and she agreed to give it a go.

Now I admit I do expect miracles but even I was stunned by the quick results. On Monday morning Linda came in glowing and said, "What are you doing on May 21? My private showing is scheduled and I want to dedicate it to you." We were both so excited. Drinking champagne at her gallery opening was probably one of the most rewarding experiences I've had in a long time. Eventually, I lost Linda, but by giving her encouragement I grew in the process. You see, I judge my own success not in dollars, but by how many people I help and encourage in my lifetime.

By taking the time to develop, coach, and guide our staff or associates, we become a stepping stone on their climb to success. If you are happy with your work right now, offer to mentor someone who needs your wisdom and direction. Look around you; chances are there is someone right now who values your wisdom and respects your talents. If you are not satisfied with your work, reach out and ask someone you respect for guidance. Most people are flattered you want their help and will be delighted to assist you. Don't be shy—ask for help. Remember, the more people you help the more you will prosper.

Everyone has a contribution to make in his or her lifetime. By doing what we love and living a happy life, we influence people all around us. You give others the gift of hope, knowledge, appreciation, or support. I challenge you to find ways to show gratitude at work and be of service to associates, customers, bosses, and peers. The spirit of gratitude and service brings passion and excitement to the workplace.

As a professional speaker, I am often approached by people who are interested in a speaking career. I always give them my number, the number of the National Speakers Association, and encourage them to call me for a brief phone appointment. Over the years, I have personally mentored several speakers who are now doing quite well as entrepreneurs. By helping them, I am giving back for all the gifts I've been given. Personally, it gives me great joy to share in their success. Plus, I truly believe we all have a responsibility to encourage others.

Many spiritual leaders over the centuries emphasize the importance of caring for others, particularly those less fortunate than ourselves. It's so easy to become self-absorbed in our problems and lose sight of how good we may have it. If you enjoy interacting with people on committees, volunteer work is very rewarding and builds our leadership skills. Whether your volunteer activities revolve around work, church, or community activities, make sure you enjoy yourself.

Also, beware of getting so involved in helping others that your personal life suffers. Remember, our family and friends may need us first.

Okay, so you're not the "joiner" type. Perhaps there's a neighbor, child, or senior citizen who needs a good listener, a kind word, or some companionship. Ask for guidance and strength from above.

With the sped up society we live in, information and technology has caused us to be more productive. Productivity is good. But I'm afraid we've also become more unavailable to our family, friends, those in need, and in some cases, even ourselves.

Sometimes when I'm busy on the road, if I have an extra ten or fifteen minutes I scan my address book and try to reconnect with dear friends from the past. Even if they may not be the initiator, I take the responsibility of keeping the relationship alive. People matter to me. By making it a goal and a priority I make the time to reach out to people.

What about you? Are you giving people the gift of you? Do you realize the awesome power you hold to make someone smile? To encourage a discouraged person? To comfort a wounded heart? To build someone's self-esteem? You make a difference.

Summary of Key Points

- Be appreciative of what you do have.
- Understand how gratitude and service to others can expedite your dreams.

■ Demonstrate appreciation and be of help to others.

■ Be grateful and of service in the workplace.

Seven Easy Ways to Demonstrate Appreciation and the Spirit of Service

1. Leave a surprise thank-you note with a cookie or piece of chocolate for a family member or an associate at work and express your gratitude.

2. Tell a waitress or salesperson they provided you with exceptional service.

3. Call up a friend or associate and leave a special message telling them how much you appreciate them. Spice it up by playing fun music in the background.

4. Ask your friend or staff at work about their weekend or challenges in their life and really *listen* and be supportive.

5. Mentor an employee or associate by taking the time to train, coach, encourage, and provide them with career guidance.

6. Thank a client, friend, or associate with a gift that keeps your name alive monthly, such as a magazine subscription or book or wine club.

7. Volunteer to head a committee at work or in your community and focus on giving back.

Exercise: Five-Minute Joy Booster

Every morning this week before you get out of bed, prop up the pillows, sit back, and take a few minutes to imagine one of your dreams. Then either say a little prayer, an affirmation,̓ or read one of the quotes at the end of this section.

Exercise: I Am Thankful

Open your Dream Big workbook and write on a new page, I Am Thankful and date it. Now list everything in your life you are thankful for—the sun, your friends, your health, your home, your favorite chair. Let the gratitude pour out of your soul. And let's never forget to thank the source of our spiritual gifts.

Exercise: I Enjoy Giving and Mentoring

In your Dream Big workbook on a new page, write I Enjoy Giving. Now list several ways you intend to give of your time, help a friend, donate, coach an associate, and so forth.

Dream Big Group Members or Partner

Each of you share a few things for which you are grateful in your life.

Message for the Spiritually Inclined

Whatever circumstances you're facing now, I'm sure you have something to be thankful for. Remember to express gratitude each day. Try the following words to express your thanks.

Dear Lord or _____, Thank you for all the blessings in my life, specifically for _____.

■ ■ ■

Because the grace of God or _____ has been given to us, we are assured that we can never fail–even if we feel we have. Each experience, whether completely successful or not, is a chance to learn and grow. With peace and love in our hearts, we gratefully say, "Thank you, God or _____, for the wonder of your grace in our lives."

—Excerpted from the *Daily Word*

PART IV

Discover the Secret to Make It Happen

An Optional Message for the Spiritually Inclined

I have never written anything I feel so strongly about as Dream Big. Through this book I am totally committed to helping you have your dream and giving you every opportunity to *choose* to succeed. After all, it is your choice.

I believe everything I have—my loving husband, speaking abilities, nice home, wonderful family and friends—is a gift from God. Every dream I've achieved in the past and will have in the future is with God's help and direction. That doesn't mean I sat around waiting, hoping things would get better. I *chose* to expect the best, *asked* for guidance, and took *action* when the opportunities arose.

Let me make one thing perfectly clear: I respect all beliefs and religions. Throughout this book, I often inserted a blank line so you can insert your own word or term for your spiritual source. Think of a bicycle wheel. There is one God (the hub) and many paths (the spokes). The closer to the hub, the closer the spokes are to each other. Over the years I've evolved from a totally I-do-it-all, positive-thinking approach, to my current I-am-divinely-guided belief. Please embrace whatever philosophy you wish.

In my own search, there's been a major shift in how I strengthened my spiritual connection. For many years I said daily affirmations, such as, "I am now a nationally known speaker." "I am now in a wonderful relationship."

One day, out of the clear blue, my inner voice, Sparkles, said, "Barbara, why don't you add, 'through the grace of God' at the end of each affirmation?" I thought to myself it was too religious-sounding, not my style. At that time I didn't even go to church. I usually prayed to the "universe." But I thought, "What if it's a special message for me? I've got nothing to lose."

With a slight adjustment, I began adding, "through the grace of God" to my daily affirmations. Within months, Bob came into my life. Then a publisher approached me about writing my first book. Coincidence, you might say. I don't think so. I began to question my entire spiritual outlook. What if I begin talking to God and Jesus each day and asking for direction? Well, I did just that. More blessings and gifts came my way. I thought, "This is amazing." Informal conversations with God became a weekly and then a daily practice. Now I can't imagine my life without this "chat" with my Friend.

I became filled with an increased feeling of well being and peace. Confident in life and in all my decisions, I made changes and took risks I never imagined.

Now it's time for you to have the life you deserve. If you have any spiritual beliefs at all, I urge you to practice the affirmations and prayers at the end of each section. Acknowledge and thank your source of strength and ask for help and direction. Remember, nothing new needs to be created to fulfill your dreams. It already exists. Just be open to receiving your gifts.

If you are reading this section with skepticism or do not believe in God or a higher power, I empathize. For seven long years I didn't believe in any spiritual connection. I remember thinking, "This is it—my life. No one's going to guide me and when it's all over that's it."

After a particularly discouraging incident that just about broke me, I cried out for help for the first time in my life. "Dear God, I know I rarely talk to You and I admit sometimes I doubt You even exist. Please help me feel the peace and happiness I seek. Please make me feel Your presence—come into my life. Fill my mind with Your words of encouragement. Talk to me and I will listen." I immediately felt an incredible sense of calm and hope. Two days later I suddenly was aware the cloud had lifted from me. I saw my way out of my problems and began taking positive steps to solve them.

Ever since that day, I have never felt alone.

Keep your mind open; you've got nothing to lose. Try some of the spiritual tips for a month or two. Say, "If You really do exist, please make Yourself known to me." Wait patiently. If you are sincere in your search and expect an answer, you won't be disappointed. Doubt and fear, however, will negate your request.

> *I guess if I had to get out my message in one sentence, it's simply this:*
>
> *Whatever you're dreaming—it's not big enough!*

Think about that. It's not big enough. So now what will you do?

The choice is yours. You can put the book away and say, "Nice message, but it won't work for me." Or you can make a decision and say, "I intend to create my future by dreaming big."

If you implement only one thing in this book, I strongly urge you to make your Dream Big board.

Next, share this book with a friend who supports you and join the Big Dream club. Don't let your excitement and desires wane. Keep the fire burning and act now.

The morning joy-booster exercise is very powerful. If you're tight on time, take three minutes instead of five each morning to focus on your dreams and ask for guidance. This special investment of your time will come back tenfold.

Of one thing I am certain. If you add the spiritual tips to the six-step process with total belief and faith, you will have your dreams and more at mach speed.

Remember, you are not alone in the journey of life. You are loved and guided each day. Ask, believe, and listen for the answers you seek. So remember…

Dream big! What's the best that can happen?

Listen to your intuition for it is your best friend.
Ignore your fears for they are your enemy.
Believe in your dreams for they are your future

—Barbara Sanfilippo

An Invitation to Join the Big Dream Club!

If you are interested in accelerating the arrival of your dreams, form a Dream Big group with three to six friends and join the Big Dream Club. By reviewing the six-step *make it happen* process at each meeting and sharing your frustrations and successes, you will create a powerful support system. An email newsletter featuring success stories and how other club members overcame challenges is in the works. Membership is free!

If you are a sales professional we also have a special Dream Big sales interest group (SIG) that focuses on using the process to exceed sales expectations.

Finally, if you simply want to be part of our club as an individual and you're not inclined to form a group that's fine. Just sign up!

Please email Barb@Romanosanfilippo.com or fax 760-738-8900 with the information requested below and become a club member now!

❑ Yes, I'd like to join your Big Dream Club individually.

❑ Yes, I'd like to join your Club and register as a Dream Big group leader.

- -

Your name: _____

Title: _____

Company: _____

Number of employees:_____

Home address:* _____

City:_____State: _____ Zip: _____

*A home address is preferable only because it typically changes less than a work address. If you prefer a work address list it above.

Home telephone ( ) _____

Fax ( ) _____

Work telephone ( ) _____

Email _____

If you work at a company, does it ever use professional speakers at management, staff or sales meetings? _____

Sales professionals only complete this section:

Type of product/service _____

Number of sales reps in your company _____

National sales manager _____

Telephone ( ) _____

Thank you!

You Can Be
in This Book!

Because I know you'll be successful, I can't wait to hear about the dreams you created. Please let me know how you used the six-step process, overcame challenges, and enjoyed your Dream Big group. Also, share words of encouragement for my readers. Your stories may be used in my revised book, Dream Big newsletter and future speeches. Please mention if you prefer to be anonymous. Also, I may want to interview you further by telephone.

The easiest way to share your comments is by signing my guest book on my Web site at www.Romanosanfilippo.com and click on Barbara Sanfilippo. Or you can mail, email, or fax me at:

Barbara Sanfilippo, CSP
2421 Oak Canyon Place ■ Escondido, CA 92025
Barb@Romanosanfilippo.com
Fax: 760-738-8900

Some of My Favorite Books

The Game of Life and How to Play It by Florence Scovell Shin

Creative Visualization by Shakti Gawain

Life Application Study Bible, New Living Translation

(After reading many personal growth and success books, I finally decided to actually try to read the Bible late in life. This translation is very modern and easy to read, and the New Testament is quite motivating. Try it—I think you'll be pleasantly surprised.)

The Daily Word, 1 year monthly subscription for $6.95 (call 800-669-0282)

Think and Grow Rich by Napoleon Hill

The Instant Millionaire by Mark Fisher

The Magic of Thinking Big by David J. Schwartz

Meditations for Women Who Do Too Much Anne Wilson Schaaf

Making Your Dream Come True and *Doing Less and Having More* by Marcia Weider

The Platinum Rule and *Charisma* by Dr. Tony Allessandra

It Only Takes a Minute to Change Your Life by William Jolley

Books and Videos Available from Rudy Ruettiger*

Rudy's Rules

Rudy's Lesson for Young Champions

Rudy & Friends

Rudy Movie

* Each item is $15.00 plus $3.00 shipping. Call Rudy International at 702-224-0391.

Order Form for More Dream Big Books and Products

Check out our web page at RomanoSanfilippo.com for more products and CDs!

Please send me the following:

_____ Copies of *DREAM BIG!: What's the Best
That Can Happen?* x $13 $ _____

                                    Subtotal $ _____

            Sales tax (California) 7.5% $ _____

                        Shipping $ 3.00 $ _____

        Add $1.75 for each additional book $ _____

                              Total due $ _____

Call us for a discount on book orders over 30 copies.

Choose one of the following options to order:

1. **Call** us toll free at 1-877-I Succeed with your credit card number.

2. Visit www.RomanoSanfilippo.com and order from the "products" section.

3. Copy this form and **fax** it with your credit card number to 760-738-8900.

4. **Email** us at Barb@Romanosanfilippo.com with your credit card number.

5. Copy this form and **mail** it to us with your credit card number or check payable to: **Barbara Sanfilippo, 2421 Oak Canyon Place, Escondido, CA 92025.**

(over)

Credit card no.:_____ Exp: _____

Name: _____

Title: _____

Home address: _____

Company name: _____

City:_____ State:_____ Zip: _____

Home telephone: ( ) _____

Work: ( ) _____

Email: _____

Fax: ( ) _____

(Allow 2 to 3 weeks for delivery.)